MIDWEST LANDSCAPE DESIGN

MIDWEST
LANDSCAPE
DESIGN

Susan McClure

PHOTOGRAPHY BY IAN ADAMS

TAYLOR PUBLISHING COMPANY ᧞ DALLAS, TEXAS

To Janet Adams,
for support above and beyond the call of duty.

Frontispiece: *A rustic arbor and pots of fuchsia welcome visitors.*

Published by Taylor Publishing Company
1550 West Mockingbird Lane
Dallas, Texas 75235
www.taylorpub.com

Library of Congress Cataloging-in-Publication Data
McClure, Susan, 1957–
    Midwest landscape design / written by Susan McClure.
      p.   cm.
    ISBN 0-87833-218-9
    1. Gardens—Middle West—Design. 2. Landscape design—Middle
West. I. Title.
    SB473.M36 1999
    712'.6'0977—dc21   98-43757
                                              CIP

Printed in the United States of America
10 9 8 7 6 5 4 3 2 1

CONTENTS

ॐ

ACKNOWLEDGMENTS

&

I applaud the busy designers who took the time to share the gardens they created. They include Pat Armstrong, Craig Bergmann, Libby Bruch, Michelle D'Arcy, Rich Eyre, Charles Freeman, Jeff Forinash, Jim Hagstrom, Doug Hoerr, June Hutson, Cliff Miller, Ken Miller, Vicki Nowicki, Brian Parsons, Steve Pattie, Kathy Stokes-Shafer, Jane Rogers, arLene Shannon, and Dana Owens. Thanks also to William Fehrenbach, James Grigsby, Peter Girard, and Doug MacCarthy.

To the garden owners, most of whom remain anonymous, thank you for inviting us into your private domain.

A standing ovation is due to photographer Ian Adams, who was always happy to go on assignment—no matter how far afield—and who always came back with just the right images.

A splashing fountain adds life to the service patio.

One

LANDSCAPE DESIGNERS AND THE DESIGN PROCESS

❧

L andscape designers are artists and scholars who turn visions into reality, shaping the look of the future with seedlings planted today. They change wide-open spaces into outdoor places for living and relaxing. They are artists, planners, craftsmen, dirt-under-the-fingernails plantsmen, plumbers, conservationists, nurserymen, plant explorers, and more.

A garden must be in proportion to its surroundings.

Garden designers strive to create a unified blend of garden structures and plants.

These are exhaustive job requirements. Those who meet them find that landscape design is not an easy profession. It requires long hours, sometimes grueling work under the hot sun, and extensive knowledge. But designers agree that theirs is a labor of love.

It is a heady experience to work hand in hand with nature, sculpting the land and molding living objects into functional art forms. Landscape designers paint the earth, not with watercolors, pastels, or other inanimate media, but with plants that make a living tapestry more complex than any fabric. The designers' landscape artistry grows and changes with time. Their creations have living beauty that reveals the activity of nature outside our sheltered doorways.

Midwest Landscape Design features twenty garden designers, all of whom call the region their home. Whether they are landscape architects, landscape designers, horticulturists, naturalists, nurserymen, or plant collectors, all are alike in one fashion: They bring their own unique styles to the landscape using a palette of plants that are ideal for the Midwest.

Their designs include gardens with great structure, outdoor rooms, and designs with formal and informal roots—all landscapes with rhythm, unity, balance, and perspective. Learning from these

A landscape designer may appear similar to an artist who paints natural images on a canvas. The difference is that the landscape designer works in the present and future simultaneously, planning ten or twenty years in advance while he or she plants today.

design professionals—and others—can open your eyes to dynamic new possibilities for your own yard.

Landscape architects are qualified to design pools and other complicated structures.

What Are Landscape Designers and Landscape Architects?

Throughout this book, you'll find several categories of designers lumped under the general term *landscape designer*. But by no means are all of these categories of designers alike. They vary dramatically in education, perspective, and technical know-how, differences you should be aware of before hiring a designer of your own.

Landscape architects have undergraduate or graduate degrees in landscape architecture. In addition, nearly every state requires landscape architects to be registered with the state. In some states, a nondegreed landscaper can be registered upon passing a test. Many are especially well versed in architecture, civil engineering, and urban planning, focusing their work on large commercial and institutional projects such as parks and office complexes. Some

Some landscape designers specialize in working with flowers, making colorful tapestries such as this blend of yarrow, purple loosestrife, and cosmos.

landscape architects can be found on the staff of a design/build landscape company or in a small practice specializing in home landscapes.

Although higher priced than most other kinds of landscape designers, landscape architects can deal with tricky changes in grade, swimming pool construction and other technical elements of construction. Many landscape architects also can render general planting plans; a smaller percentage are superb plantsmen able to provide detailed garden plans for perennial borders, herb gardens, and other specialized projects.

Landscape designers are a varied lot who can practice their craft without any special credentials. One way to find an experienced designer is to look for one that is certified by the Association of Professional Landscape Designers.

Many landscape designers come from horticultural backgrounds, using their intimate knowledge of plants as a basis for design. Some are independent freelancers; others are on the staffs of design/build landscape companies, nurseries, botanical gardens, or arboretums. Some landscape designers are self-taught, having created their own great gardens at home and then branched out to take on outside clients.

Make sure that any designer you hire has the background necessary to tackle your job. If you want a detailed perennial garden, a horticulturist-designer may be ideal. If you want an innovative approach to using your yard, someone with an artistic background may be especially appropriate. Either way, the designer should have a portfolio of prior projects to show you and satisfied customers to offer as referrals.

Landscape designers work in several ways. Some, such as horticulturists on the staffs of botanical gardens, prefer to consult. For an hourly fee, they will come to your yard and give you ideas and possibly an informal sketch of how you can lay out the landscape. Some also provide a written report and plant lists, which can help you follow their instructions.

Scale drawings, such as this secret garden plan by architect Jane Smedley, provide specifics needed for garden visualization and installation.

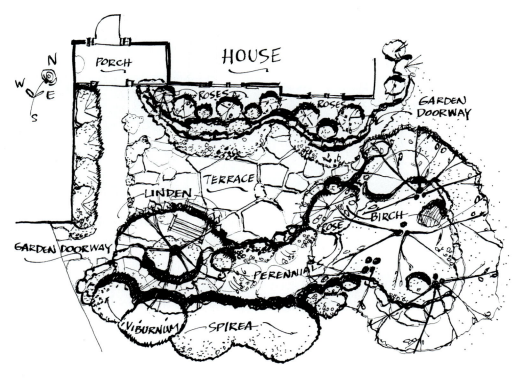

Design/build firms can build garden gates and plant them with flowering vines like 'Mrs. Annette Henter' wisteria.

Other freelance designers may provide an initial consultation and then draw a scale landscape plan, a blueprint for the landscape construction. It takes more time to measure the yard and to draft this kind of plan, but leaves no question as to what must be done.

Freelance designers usually charge by the hour for design work and estimate installation separately. Some designers charge a higher fee for initial consultation and then drop their rates for later drafting. Some freelancers also subcontract the construction or supervise your landscape team, ensuring that their ideas are properly implemented.

Design/build firms, which do both plans and installation, may offer you a free design, building the cost of that service into the construction. Instead of charging by the hour, some will charge by the project, making changes without additional expense. Some firms also have a maintenance division, for tending landscapes that they design and install.

Nurserymen, professionals primarily involved with growing plants, may also dabble in design. They can be worth seeking out if you want a specialized kind of garden, such as one of dwarf conifers or herbs. This kind of landscape designer can supply tried-and-true plants as well as unusual ones, along with ideas for using them in a garden. Some of the best nurserymen also plant their own display gardens, where you can get ideas for your own yard.

Regardless of which kind of designer you use, a good landscape design is not inexpensive. It's best not to skimp on the cost of the design itself—it will be your guide. If you can't afford to install a proposed design, you can break the project into phases to tackle as your finances allow. You also can do a portion of it yourself—scouting out your own plants on sale, planting your own perennial and herb gardens, taking care of tasks like watering, weeding, and mulching.

A designer specializing in edible ornamental gardens may introduce you to gourmet lettuces like 'Freckles'.

Understanding Your Landscape Needs

For a landscape of any size or style to work, it must harmonize with your lifestyle, provide beautiful scenes when viewed from indoors and out, and cater to your special interests—furnishing a place for parties, swimming, outdoor cooking, children's play, quiet reading, or privacy. It should beautify your yard, framing the house and reflecting your favorite colors. A handsome, mature landscape also can increase your property value by as much as 40 percent.

Adding a fountain to a patio will fill it with the music of splashing water.

All of these benefits take planning, the kind that professional landscape designers can help with. You should spend a little time considering what you want to accomplish with your yard, either before you hire a designer or in consultation with the designer.

Sometimes a designer will provide a questionnaire to help you focus your thoughts and to give him or her a personal blueprint to follow. These questionnaires often address concepts such as the following:

    ❧ What size of outdoor gathering areas, such as patios, decks, and terraces, will you need? The answer will be influenced by the size of your family and circle of friends and by how much outdoor entertaining you do.

    ❧ How much room should be devoted to play areas? Play areas will change, depending on the ages of your children. Younger children's playgrounds may later be transformed

Left: Cozy patios are well suited for intimate gatherings or small families.

Below: A swimming pool is a great place to get your aerobic exercise and can also make the yard more beautiful.

If you want to grow your own food, have an attractive kitchen garden worked into your landscape plan.

into volleyball courts or other areas conducive to teenage play. Does your family have a special sports interest and need a basketball court or a putting green? Do you have the time to enjoy and maintain a swimming pool or hot tub?

❧ How much privacy do you need? What views of the street, the compost pile, or the neighbor's garage need to be screened with a wall of greenery? Would it be helpful to filter out area noise with a berm? Do you want an especially private area for reading, sunbathing, or talking?

❧ How can you enhance existing scenery? What views of a nearby creek, woodland, or a beautiful old oak, for instance, are attractive and should be framed by the landscape design?

❧ Do you have special gardening interests? Do you want to grow your own vegetables and herbs? Do you like fresh-cut flowers for indoors? Do you want an intricate perennial border? Are you willing to devote the time—and do you have the knowledge—to keep up these kinds of high-maintenance gardens, or will you need to hire extra help to do so?

❧ How can you use your landscape to minimize energy costs? Can you use a wall of evergreens to shield your home from cold northwest winds? Would you like a shade tree on the south or west side of your bedroom or living room to cut the hot summer sun and reduce air-conditioning bills?

Design Elements

Designers juggle a variety of fundamentals to put together a landscape design that is beautiful, effective, and appropriate for the site. Here is a sampling of their tools—tools as important as a gardener's shovel and hoe.

❧ **Space**: This is the area encompassed by each portion of the landscape and the landscape as a whole. It influences the sizes of beds and plants within the beds.

❧ **Proportion**: Plants and garden features that are in scale with the space give the landscape a comfortable feeling. A well-proportioned small yard may have a small crabapple, dwarf viburnums, and a modestly sized perennial garden. A large yard will need big, sweeping beds; large masses of similar flowers; and big, bold trees to retain a sense of proportion.

❧ **Line**: Created by walks, walls, bed outlines, trees, and the like, landscape lines can be vertical or horizontal, straight or curved. They have a strong influence on landscape aesthetics, draw the eye through the yard, and help to tie sections together.

A red-leafed banana plant makes a bold focal point for this large garden of sunflowers and snapdragons.

Aged brick has a warm earthy color, while stone can be brighter and more iridescent.

❧ **Texture**: Provided by building materials and plants, textures can range from rugged and irregular to smooth and delicate. A design needs enough textural similarity for continuity but also enough variation for interesting contrast.

❧ **Color**: Bricks, walls, leaves, flowers, fruit, and stems all have color. Pleasing combinations of harmonious or contrasting colors make a strong impression.

❧ **Balance**: Equal weight or interest on both sides of any landscape or garden makes the plan look stable, consistent, and in harmony. Formal gardens often have symmetrical or mirror-image plantings, with the same planting repeated on each side of a central access line. Informal gardens may be asymmetrical, perhaps pairing a tree on one side of a theoretical divide with a cluster of shrubs on the other for similar impact with different elements.

Repetition of yellow-flowered marsh marigolds gives this garden scene rhythm.

❧ **Dominance**: A prominent object, such as a sculpture, doorway, or weeping conifer, or an area of the garden such as a winding walk or exciting plant combination can attract the eye and become a center of attention.

❧ **Rhythm**: Repetition of a plant, color, texture, line, or other element throughout the garden or landscape gives it continuity. Rhythm draws elements of the landscape together, creating one beautiful picture.

Two

THE MIDWEST, A UNIQUE REGION

The Midwest, with farm fields rich in corn, winter wheat, and soybeans, is famous both as America's heartland and as the breadbasket of the country. The region's compatibility with agriculture bodes well for Midwestern landscapes, which will prosper if designed to be in harmony with the climate and native soil.

Compared with coastal climates and warmer areas of the country, the Midwestern climate may

Japanese primroses and azaleas make a dynamic spring show.

Right: Growing tomatoes is a Midwestern gardening specialty.

Below right: Fragrant-flowered hyacinths make spring special but usually require replacing each autumn to perform reliably.

Below: Summer brings brilliant blooms on roses like 'L.D. Braithwaite'.

Fountain grass, chrysanthemums, sunflowers, and the last blooms of a butterfly bush fill the author's autumn garden with color.

appear rigorous; in reality it is generous in each of its four seasons. There is a well-defined spring, summer, fall, and winter—an ever-changing cycle that reminds us of nature's powerful presence.

Spring begins with a slow awakening of crocus, forsythias, magnolias, lilacs, daffodils, and, in woodland gardens, with wild-flowers such as trilliums, jack-in-the-pulpits, and mayapples. It ends amid an abundance of spring showers, with a flourish of flowers on peonies, crabapples, and rhododendrons. Spring in the Midwest garden cannot be tied to an official calendar season. It usually starts in March or April (when the weather begins to warm) and generally ends in May (around the time of the last spring frost).

Summer is usually draped in humidity and often accompanied by short droughts. Although the Midwest's summer heat can be oppressive, it inspires bountiful crops of zucchinis and tomatoes, lavish marigolds and petunias, and other warm-season classics. Midwestern prairie plants, such as sunflowers, coneflowers, and blazing stars, thrive regardless of Midwestern heat or dry spells, making them naturals for the summer garden.

Even in winter the landscape can be attractive.

Marking the end of the growing season, autumn may be the most beautiful quarter of all. Early autumn brings warm days and cool evenings colored with asters, chrysanthemums, and the lacy, painted heads of ornamental kale. Leaves on maples, dogwoods, viburnums, and other deciduous species lose their green overcoats, revealing scarlet, golden, and orange pigments below. After heavy frost paints leaves and limbs with silver, there remain golden ornamental grasses and bright berries on gray dogwoods and viburnums.

Winter is the season that allows Midwestern gardeners to rest and watch the winter landscape caped in white, gray, or brown. A well-planned landscape will show hints of vivid bark on red-twig

In early spring, snowdrops may flower despite a blanket of snow.

dogwoods or green-stemmed Japanese kerria and evergreen foliage on plants such as hollies and junipers. Winter also is time for the garden catalogues to arrive, bringing bright promises and exciting new ideas for planting in the spring season to come.

Throughout the seasons, the landscape is continually changing—flowing from buds into flowers and then fruit. It is never stationary, always following the rhythm of the seasons. Midwestern gardeners, likewise, soon learn to read the weather and make the most of the region's gifts.

The Nature of the Midwest

Beyond its generally warm summers and cold winters, Midwestern weather is irregular. Understanding its changeability develops a sense of resilience and patience that comes from knowing that in time, all things will come—cold and warm, wet and dry.

Another distinctive characteristic of the Midwest is its wild areas and spreading countryside. Images, structures, lines, and forms found in these areas can be duplicated in the cultivated landscape. Inspiration awaits those who can appreciate mixed hardwood forests, prairies of tall grasses and golden flowers, meadows, rural roadsides, bogs, and dunes.

Throughout the region, country roads ramble past farm fields, with their neat rows of corn or soybeans stretching toward the horizon. Reflecting an insistence on neatness and organization, a farmer's ethic, this motif carries through to manicured Midwestern lawns and homes neatly edged in rows of sheared shrubs and tidy lines of geraniums and tulips. The typical vegetable garden, with rows of beans, carrots, and lettuce, follows suit.

Opposite: The Midwest is famous for its productivity.

Below: Wild lupines spread across the Indiana Dunes.

Garden forget-me-nots are Eurasian flowers that have escaped and grow like wild in America.

Fallow fields, juxtaposed with tidy fields of crops, show a wilder aspect of the region, a contrasting view of increasing importance as a landscape inspiration. Covered with white, cloud-like clusters of daisy fleabane (once thought to repel fleas), glistening blades of grass, and brown seed spikes of dock, the fields make a beautiful tapestry that provides inspiration for prairie gardens, meadow gardens, and naturalistic perennial gardens. While the blend is seemingly random, there is rhythm to the groupings that many find appealing.

Some of the most common rural plants and roadside plants are not native to the Midwest, however; in fact, they are not native to the United States. Plants such as Eurasian chicory, Queen-Anne's-lace, and Canada thistle are such successful invaders of roadside and field that they have become tied to the Midwestern image.

Brilliant orange trumpets and fountain-like, leafy clumps of orange daylilies duel poetically with the jagged stems, ragged leaves, and cool blue flowers of chicory. Such striking contrasting colors and textures can inspire similar combinations—butterfly weed and balloon flower, or stokesia and crocosmia.

Regardless of the nearly ubiquitous presence of weedy invaders, each region has its own unique flora, plants whose birthright on this soil long precedes our own. Some conservationists, including Pat Armstrong and Brian Parsons, use these floristic fingerprints to make gardens of native species. The gardens provide a unique look that reflects the special nature of each place.

A landscape designer with a flair for expressing the spirit of an area can employ patterns and plants from the region. Here are some common ecosystems that you might want to emulate.

Prairies

One of the images often associated with the Midwest and Great Plains is the prairie, with its ocean of grasses such as big and little bluestem and prairie dropseed. Intermingled are a variety of prairie flowers, most of which concentrate their bloom in summer or fall.

Prairies' immensity, natural diversity, and productivity long have captivated those who have beheld them. Frank Lloyd Wright based his prairie style of architecture on the grasslands originally seen around his rural Wisconsin birthplace. Instead of imposing an alien house design on the land, he designed houses tailored to the environment. With the prairie in mind, he conceived of a low, spreading house that echoed the sweep of the prairie, with walls that protected inhabitants from the elements but didn't distance them from the world outdoors.

Jens Jensen also recognized the aesthetic value of the prairie. An early 1900s landscape designer, Jensen was superintendent of various Chicago-area parks and founder of The Clearing, a northern Wisconsin school that connects designers with nature. He was also an early proponent of natural landscaping and prairie styles of gardens.

The wide blue sky and the flowers of this golden compass plant provide natural color contrast.

"Landscaping is just being born," he wrote in 1939, "and its birthright is the soul of the out-of-doors. The world is rich in landscapes in harmony with soil and climatic conditions. In the virgin forest you can read the story of creation . . . there are a multitude of ideas for the fertile mind to work with and shape into something that will inspire the race with a spiritual force for real accomplishments in the realm of art." (From: Grese. *Jens Jensen*. © 1992 by Robert E. Grese. Johns Hopkins University Press.)

Once self-maintaining systems, prairies held woody plants at bay with droughty summers and occasional fires. Today prairies have a more limited scope, but can be seen and enjoyed in prairie parks that have arisen to preserve or re-create this once-thriving ecosystem.

Opposite: Gray-headed coneflowers and wild bergamot mingle with prairie grasses.

Below: Prairie flowers mingle in a cultivated meadow garden.

Opposite: Hardy geraniums, woodland phlox, and naturalized forget-me-nots will grow in shade or at a woodland edge.

If you don't see actual prairies, you are certain to find native prairie plants along country roadsides, beside farm fields, or rambling along fencerows. Wild bergamot, with shaggy clusters of lavender flowers, has wonderfully fragrant leaves used to make herbal tea. Unlike its relative, bee balm, which thrives in moist soils, wild bergamot tolerates dry prairie and hillside soils.

Purple coneflower, black-eyed Susan, prairie blazing-star, and the common sunflower are among other prairie natives that have become standards in perennial gardens throughout the Midwest and beyond. Easy to grow in average, well-drained soils and attractive to butterflies and birds, they have much to recommend.

For specifics on prairie gardens, see Chapter 3, Prairie Style, beginning on page 35.

Eastern Woodlands

Mixed hardwood forests stretch through Ohio and into Indiana, Illinois, eastern Missouri, Iowa, and southern Minnesota, with a variety of species that are easily used in Midwestern landscapes. Mature woodlands form vegetative layers, with cool, green tree canopies of maples, oaks, hickories, beeches, and other deciduous species spreading a ceiling across the land. Smaller trees and shrubs, including dogwood, redbud, and witch hazel, form a lower layer, while spring-blooming wildflowers stretch along the forest floor. Summer and autumn bloomers may cluster at the woodland edge or in well-lit openings where a tree has fallen and left a gap in the canopy. Ferns, ground-covering partridgeberries, and occasional stands of primitive club moss can color the forest floor with greenery much of the year.

The great white trillium can be a showy spring wildflower in woods where deer browsing is minimal.

"Observe wild wooded groves to see how trees grow in relation to each other—a natural spacing that is wonderful to re-create in the landscape. You'll find that the grove is defined as much by the open spaces between trees as by the trees themselves. These spaces appeal to our inner child, the persona at the core of our being who still marvels at the wild world. It also speaks to

The natural spacing of woodland trees can have a comforting look.

the vestiges of primal man in us who lived in the forest," says landscape designer Cliff Miller of Lake Bluff, Illinois.

Miller and other designers share ideas for woodland garden designs, appropriate even for shady suburban lots, in Chapter 4, Woodland Gardens.

Northern Hardwood Forest

Found in much of Michigan as well as parts of Wisconsin and Minnesota, the northern hardwood forest is home to beech trees, maples, and paper birches, along with Canada hemlocks. The striking blend of light and dark and the dense groves of evergreens are two hallmarks of these forests that can be duplicated in residential landscapes. Unfortunately, light-barked paper birches don't always adapt well to warmer climates, even in lower parts of the Midwest. Heat and less-than-ideal soil can stress the trees, making them easy prey for bronze birch borers, which tunnel into wood, where they are hard to control, and which can kill a tree. (Adapting

Variegated Solomon's-seal, a Eurasian native, arises beneath a grove of gray birch trees.

the soil for a paper birch can minimize stress. Look for a technique recommended by Cliff Miller on page 60.)

Certain wildflowers and ground covers grow in the typically acidic soil found in northern woodlands and make attractive companions for birches, hemlocks, and other woodland species. One notable ground cover is wintergreen, a creeping shrub with mint-scented oval leaves, white flowers, and red berries that linger all winter. In moist, open areas, there may be rich peat bogs of

*Raised beds can improve poor
or waterlogged soil.*

sphagnum moss, from which Canadian peat is harvested, or sedges
and reeds, from which Michigan peat is harvested.

Climatic and Other Site Characteristics

A landscape will work to its fullest only if it is tailored to the land
and location. Weather, soil, and sunlight are basic considerations.

Weather and Soil

Gardening is a hobby that goes hand in glove with nature and her
cohorts—earth, wind, and weather. Once you've lived in a region
for a couple of years, you'll learn how to deal with your soil, which
can vary from stark, dry sand to dense clay.

You'll also begin to see that the predictably erratic weather can
supply droughts or excessive rain, late frosts, frigid winters or mild
ones, all without much warning.

It is the landscape designer's job to make sure the landscape is
prepared to weather any adversity. Designers may call for raised

beds or drainage systems where native soils are easily waterlogged. In cold climates or sites exposed to strong winter winds, designers will call for extra-hardy plants.

Finding appropriate plants begins with determining which zone you live in according to the U.S. Department of Agriculture's hardiness map, which divides the country into regions based on winter low temperatures. Unless you like to take chances, any perennial plant in your landscape should be rated hardy in your climatic zone.

The Midwest covers four hardiness zones (see map). In Zone 6, which stretches across southern parts of Ohio, Indiana, Illinois, Missouri, and Kansas, annual minimum temperatures average 0 to -10 degrees F. In Zone 5, in parts of Ohio, Indiana, Illinois, Missouri, Kansas, Michigan, Iowa, Nebraska, and Wisconsin, annual minimum temperatures can average -10 to -20 degrees F. Zone 4, in northern Michigan, Iowa, Nebraska, most of South Dakota, southern Minnesota, and central Wisconsin, has annual minimum temperatures that average -20 to -30 degrees F. Zone 3, where annual minimum temperatures average -30 to -40 degrees F, encompasses northern portions of North Dakota, Wisconsin, Minnesota, and Michigan.

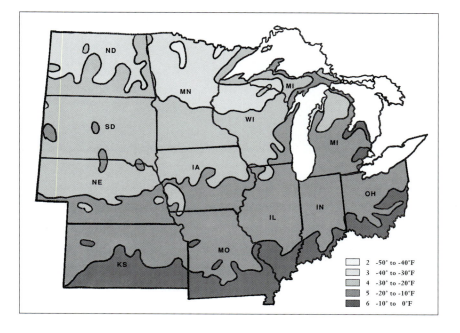

Oakleaf hydrangeas thrive in light shade.

When it comes to plants and gardening, however, no rule is unbreakable. This is particularly true with generalizations about hardiness zones and other aspects of the Midwestern climate. Sheltered planting areas beside a basement wall, "banana belts" along the shores of the Great Lakes, and sheltered city gardens will have milder winters than surrounding areas. This is called the microclimate effect. Another interesting phenomenon arises in snowbelts. Although these are cold climates, their heavy snow cover insulates plants that are low-growing or lying dormant underground. In fact, those plants often have better winter survival than plants in similar or slightly milder climates with little snow.

Sunshine

Plants are solar-powered beings that must be drafted into the landscape according to their preferences for sun, shade, or conditions in between. For a garden of sun-loving plants—roses, geraniums, and lavender, for instance—plant where there is at least six hours of sun each day. Plants that tolerate light shade or partial sun will grow where there is four to six hours of direct sun. For sites with less than four hours of sun per day, stick with shade-loving or shade-tolerant plants.

Using a local designer who employs a palette of plants that are tried and true and which thrive in other local landscapes can save you from having to balance all of these factors against plant needs.

Portable potted plants are especially easy to protect from adverse weather.

Three

PRAIRIE STYLE

❧

he sunny side of the Midwest may be embodied in the wide-open blue skies, vast expanses of grass, and brilliant flowers of the prairies that once stretched through the Great Plains to Indiana.

With a look that's unique and tranquil, flat surfaces of prairie-grass blades shimmer silvery in the sun while the undersides stay a deep sea-green. The dueling colors fluctuate as breezes blow.

At Jim Hagstrom's home, Russian sage mingles with native black-eyed Susans, beard-tongue, and bee balm.

The prairie is one of the most distinctive ecosystems in the Midwest.

Although much of the native prairie has been lost to farm fields and residential developments, prairie plants are finding new homes—in prairie and meadow gardens that are gaining popularity across the Midwest. These gardens, for all of their natural simplicity, have multiple advantages. They are planted with beautiful blends of native plants that grow and naturalize easily, requiring little upkeep once the garden is established.

While sometimes slow to color in spring, prairie gardens gain momentum once summer arrives, painting large or small areas with green grasses, golden sunflowers, and mixed purples, blues, and reds. In autumn, instead of cutting old plants back and hauling them to the compost pile, gardeners leave naturalized prairie gardens standing. The grass plumes turn golden while the chocolate-brown seed heads of flowers add spice and attract a variety of birds.

Unlike lawns, which demand regular mowing and absorb more time and money in ongoing maintenance than any other landscape

Prairie grasses add rippling life to a garden.

element, prairie-style gardens need only a single mowing or burning, in early spring, each year.

The golden flowers of compass plant stretch up toward the sky.

Most of us will never give up our lawns, but it is becoming more popular to reduce the size of the lawn, devoting an edging strip or side yard to a prairie-style planting. Even the Garden Club of America has begun advocating this kind of conservation-minded garden design.

"Use native trees, shrubs, and ground covers or native grasses and wildflowers that are already well-adapted to the environment in your region. They will require less fertilizer, fewer pesticides (probably none at all!), less watering, and less maintenance," the Garden Club of America says in its brochure *The New American Lawn*.

These kinds of gardens offer other benefits as well, the club says. "Landscape fragmentation and loss of biodiversity have become major biospheric issues, issues that can be addressed by moving away from monocultures like lawns of only grass."

Prairie gardens address many ecological issues in an easygoing way. They expand the foundation of the food web, feeding birds such as beautiful indigo buntings and prairie dwellers such as the

A grass path separates Holden Arboretum's cultivated butterfly garden from the butterfly meadow.

Eastern meadowlark. For migratory songbirds far from their home, a seed-rich prairie oasis can provide food and shelter amid a desert of sterile lawns.

Naturalized goldenrods, beard-tongues, and other wildflowers nourish butterflies and other nectar-feeding creatures. A butterfly meadow at Holden Arboretum in Kirtland, Ohio, attracts more than a dozen species of butterflies with lush groves of foxglove beard-tongue, shasta daisies, wild bee balm, purple and pink coneflowers, brown-eyed Susan, and black-eyed Susan.

The butterfly meadow is divided from a carefully cultivated butterfly garden by a wide grass path. The butterfly garden resembles a classic perennial garden, with clumps of perennials separated

Prairies offer wide-open spaces, bright sunshine, and an unhindered view of the sky and horizon beyond. With a similar liberating ambiance, prairie gardens release gardeners from the drudgery of lawn maintenance—spraying, mowing, fertilizing, and watering.

by mulch openings. It is unique, however, because of its nectar-rich garden flowers, such as 'Butterfly Blue' pincushion flower, 'Jean Davis' lavender, dwarf bluestar, turtlehead, and 'Souvenir d'André Chaudron' catmint.

While butterflies do visit these flowers and are especially fond of 'Souvenir d'André Chaudron' catmint, designer Brian Parsons finds more butterflies in the meadow garden. Its thick growth and interwoven flowers and grasses provide a variety of shady shelters that butterflies need.

While many landscape designers can create prairie-style gardens, a smaller number specialize in prairies of native plants. This chapter is devoted to the work of Jim Hagstrom, a landscape architect in Minnesota and creator of many outstanding prairie gardens. You'll also learn about a suburban prairie garden created by Pat

Daisies and foxglove beard-tongue feed butterflies in late spring.

Armstrong (see page 48). Brian Parsons, Holden Arboretum naturalist and designer, also is involved in prairie design issues.

(see page 48)

Opposite: This prairie garden is framed by the driveway and house.

Working in Harmony With the Environment

Jim Hagstrom's Savanna Designs office in the quaint village of Lake Elmo, Minnesota, must be approached through a garden that hints at Hagstrom's design philosophy.

It is a gravel garden entered under a clematis-covered arbor and centered on a low fountain, shaped similarly to a fleur-de-lis. Surrounding the fountain and broad gravel paths are clusters of large prairie herbs—gray-headed coneflower and big and little bluestem grass. The garden is simple and serene, with a natural beauty that needs no further enhancement.

While Hagstrom works with a broad range of landscape styles, he is best known for his work with native plants.

"People tend to think that a beautiful garden always takes the form of an English garden, and lose sight of the beauty all around them in nature. Illuminating natural beauty is the cutting edge of landscape design now, and ironically, one of the leaders even in America is British designer John Brookes," Hagstrom said.

Brookes, an internationally renowned garden designer, teacher, and author, likes to mold gardens to the existing terrain to emphasize the uniqueness of each natural setting. He often replaces high-maintenance lawns with wilder gardens of daffodils, forget-me-nots, and other flowers capable of naturalizing. He is a proponent of dry gardens, which are beds of gravel (used for sitting areas or walks) surrounded and softened by self-seeding herbs and perennials.

Hagstrom has worked with Joan Nassauer, a former University of Minnesota professor now at the University of Michigan, who has studied American landscape ethics. She has found that a neat, well-kept suburban yard with a pristine lawn and clipped shrubs is a characteristic most people associate with being a "good neighbor." Prairie-type gardens can be integrated with elements of traditional suburban yards to create an interesting but well-tended look.

"The placement of plants and hard, built elements can make wilder, ecologically diverse gardens fit our long-seated cultural expectations," says Hagstrom, who is also an adjunct professor of

This mailbox anchors a prairie planting of bee balm and butterfly weed.

landscape architecture at the University of Minnesota. "For example, a prairie planting spreading alone across a yard could be mistaken for a vacant meadow. But if you enclose it within a white rail fence, it is framed and can be perceived as a natural thing of beauty."

The traditional landscape with a large lawn and clipped yews employs only a limited number of plants, which tend to look the same throughout the year—an effect that is calming, reliable, and stable. This is a sharp contrast to the rich diversity of plant species in prairie gardens, and the difference can seem alien, even threatening. Anchor the prairie with classical structures to counteract this reaction, Hagstrom advises. Building wild gardens around lawns or beside geometric paths and sculptures makes them easy to accept.

Coordinating plant placement also gives the prairie garden needed structure. Designers add stability to a landscape by clustering perennials and grasses in clumps or larger sweeps, painting bold strokes of color on the landscape as is commonly done in perennial gardens, and using careful tiering of plant heights, building from short to tall.

"I don't merely scatter seed in an ecologist's fashion, without a design intent," Hagstrom says.

A Country Prairie Garden

There may be no more appropriate place for a prairie garden than a Minnesota country farmhouse, where Hagstrom has crafted a prairie garden at the entryway and a prairie replica behind the house. The entry garden is designed to be particularly showy throughout the summer and fall. Its structure is intimately linked to the house, enhancing the architecture and welcoming guests. The back yard is restored so that it is similar to prairies found in Minnesota before the arrival of European colonists. It is allowed to run free, drifting and changing as the species within it mingle and blend into a working ecosystem. The entire property received an Honor Award from the Minnesota chapter of the American Society of Landscape Architects in 1996.

The house, which Hagstrom calls "indigenous Midwestern architecture," is uniquely angular, with two jutting wings facing forward and with intriguing windows set in varying patterns. A circular gravel drive passes a brawny barn and pastured herds of Norwegian Fjord horses and Scottish Highland cows before arriving at the house.

A wide walk leading to the front door is made of aggregate, forming a transition between the gravel drive and the house. It is marked with inlaid lines that draw the eye to the house. Beside the drive, the walk widens to accommodate a large stone planter, filled with a mix of classic ornamentals and prairie natives such as dusty miller, 'Vera Jameson' sedum, and prairie dropseed.

Purple coneflowers bring color to a prairie garden that terminates in a more traditional foundation planting.

Purple and gray-headed coneflowers mingle with little bluestem in front of a rustic porch.

The naturalized entryway garden forms a neatly edged teardrop-shaped area beside the front walk and fills the center of the circular drive. It provides a perfect, free-flowing contrast to the structured lines of the house and courtyard.

Bold geometric sweeps of purple and gray-headed coneflowers with their backswept florets of purple and gold blend with prairie grasses and a statuesque, three-trunked river birch with bark of peeling cinnamon. Self-seeded black-eyed Susans spread around the perimeter, where they seem to thrive, and purple spikes of liatris emerge here and there. Despite the color these flowers offer, Hagstrom is especially fond of little bluestem, which grows in solid emerald clumps that turn golden in fall and winter.

"When a garden has good 'bones,' you can get pretty wild with the plantings, using natives that change with the seasons and attract butterflies and birds. Most important of all, in my mind, is to make a connection to the land and the place, instead of planting another generic landscape that could be seen anywhere across the country," Hagstrom says.

MIXING PRAIRIE PLANTS AND CULTIVATED PERENNIALS

Landscape architect Jim Hagstrom likes to mix cultivated plants with Midwestern prairie natives, increasing the range of colors and textures available for designs. At his own home entryway, he mingles large clumps of prairie dropseed, black-eyed Susans, Joe-Pye weed, and gray-headed coneflowers with cultivated selections such as Russian sage, violet sage, and 'Autumn Joy' sedum.

In addition to the front courtyard, the bones of this landscape include a burly porch made of mammoth timbers and a tiered, backyard deck that overlooks a prairie spreading for several acres down a slight slope to farm fields beyond. Five-foot-wide, close-cropped paths move in curving lines through the prairie, adding further structure to the landscape and inviting people to wander amid the shoulder-high flowers.

This back yard is devoted to an even larger prairie planting that attracts birds, butterflies, and other wildlife.

A Backyard Prairie Border

Even a conservative landscape can benefit from a touch of natural splendor with a prairie-type border, island bed, or edging. If kept in private areas of the yard, it can be reserved for personal enjoyment without concern for public comment.

In this role, the prairie garden can serve a number of functions. The taller grasses and wildflowers form a summer screen, separating different areas of the landscape. With billowing foliage, they can soften the harsh lines of solid fences or plain walls. They can even provide a source of flowers for the dining room table, as coneflowers, blazing stars, asters, and many other prairie natives make delightful and long-lasting cut flowers.

A prairie garden forms a naturalized landscape divider at a three-acre property in White Bear Lake, Minnesota, dividing a patio that spans the rear of the house from an expansive beach-front lawn.

A prairie walkway emerges from a formal patio.

The prairie planting skirts the brick patio, a classical structure with a timber pergola and bed of phlox and yarrow on one side. A wooden boardwalk rises several feet above the downward-sloping yard and cuts in a gentle arc through the center of a dramatic prairie planting.

Tall, thick stands of big bluestem and switch grass make a feathery, green wall topped with billowing reddish-brown plumes. Touches of color—gray-headed coneflower, anise hyssop, Culver's root—brighten the verdant serenity. The prairie ends at a little grove of river birch, where the boardwalk leads to an open lawn beneath a spreading oak tree. Beyond is a hammock, strung beneath two trees near a beach house and blue waters peppered with sailboats.

A grove of river birch marks the end of the prairie boardwalk.

A Suburban Prairie

Nature lovers or those who simply disdain lawn mowing may dream about turning an entire suburban yard into a prairie, but few people follow through. That this can be done, and done well, is

Pat Armstrong developed this prairie restoration using seeds gathered in Illinois and Wisconsin.

proven by the wild-spirited prairie that naturalist and designer Pat Armstrong has developed in her Naperville, Illinois, back yard, which measures one-third of an acre. Her yard is a beautiful tapestry of flowers and grasses through most of the year and is used as a prototype for the prairie resurgence all around Chicago.

In 1983, Armstrong started the prairie by tilling the soil and finding appropriate plants. Unwilling to use purchased plants from other parts of the country, Armstrong collected three burlap bags of prairie plant seeds from around Chicago and in nearby Wisconsin. She also started her own seedlings of prairie dropseed and pale purple coneflowers, which dominate the garden. Selecting plants native to a bur-oak savanna, she ensured that the prairie could withstand alkaline soil and occasional summer droughts typical of the area.

Today there are 300 native plant species in this small area, a gold mine for a botanist and an exciting place to explore for any gardener.

Only a few non-native invaders, such as dandelions and Kentucky bluegrass, have to be routed out from time to time. She renews growth of desirable species by burning the prairie in March, with permission from Naperville. Besides pruning out suckers of sumac, gray dogwood, and wild plums, little other maintenance is necessary, she says.

The garden spreads across Armstrong's entire yard, stopping at the sidewalk and mowed right-of-way along a perimeter creek. Scattered shrub thickets and an evergreen windbreak blend with prairie grasses and wildflowers. The garden is divided by stone paths that allow close inspection of the grasses and flowers within. Taller grasses and flowers, originally started near the rear of the yard, have mingled with lower plants toward the front.

There is a small lawn immediately behind the house, but it is planted in naturally low-growing buffalo grass and side-oats grama.

Spring bloom begins with cleft phlox, violets, columbines, shooting-stars, prairie and early buttercups, prairie smoke, and lousewort. The flowering accelerates from this point on with a smorgasbord that includes butterfly weed, black-eyed Susan, pale purple coneflower, prairie dock, prairie dropseed, big bluestem, and aromatic aster. Fall and winter remain an interesting medley of dried grasses and seedpods, which attract many birds and other animals that feed on the plants.

It is a garden that pleases Armstrong, her neighbors, and her clients, who often drop by for inspiration.

Pat Armstrong is a Midwestern trendsetter in the use of native plants.

Starting a Prairie Garden

Starting and tending a prairie garden is a different kind of gardening, best approached with advice from prairie experts like Jim Hagstrom and Pat Armstrong.

Purple coneflowers mix with baptisia and bee balm.

❧ When starting a prairie, place seedlings grown in 4-inch pots a foot apart. They will begin to put on a show within a year. Seed-started prairies take several years to become established. They should be sown during late spring or summer, if you can irrigate the entire area, when temperatures are warm enough for prompt germination. Armstrong also recommends late fall seeding.

❧ To eliminate weeds in new prairies, mow a couple of times the first year with the mower set 4 to 6 inches high. (The prairie will only grow to about 2 inches high.) Also, pull out obvious weeds such as dandelions, Canada thistle, and quackgrass.

❧ Leave the garden standing in the fall, cutting, mowing, or burning plants down in spring.

"Cleaning up bronzed plants in fall caters only to people's sense of neatness; plants don't need it. They thrive on fallen organic matter, and birds feed on the seeds," Hagstrom says.

Four

WOODLAND GARDENS

꒰

idwestern woodlands are woven with handsome sugar and red maples, silver-trunked beeches, shaggy-barked hickories, acorn-bearing oaks, and other native deciduous trees. The woodland is stratified, with the taller species towering over layers of lower-growing plants—small flowering trees and shrubs such as viburnums, redbuds, dogwoods, and serviceberries. Where shade trees are mature and the

Self-seeding forget-me-nots add extra spring color to a wild lawn.

Wild columbine and dwarf crested iris spread across a rich forest floor.

soil is rich and moist, the woodland floor will be carpeted with spring ephemerals, wild-flowers that bloom early and then often fade back to the ground by midsummer.

The bell-shaped flowers of Virginia blue-bells, large open-faced trillium blossoms, and showy clusters of petite, white rue anemone greet spring while the tree leaves are expanding. The summer scene features feathery ferns and umbrella-shaped leaves of mayapples growing around rocks and fallen logs. Occasional splashes of color come from red cardinal flowers in moist clearings near a creek, while tall blue spikes of lobelia and white spikes of black snakeroot stand tall near the woodland edge. In late summer or autumn, sunlit openings are likely to be filled with flowering woodland goldenrods or asters.

Those lucky enough to have a mature woods in their yard can weave the area with winding paths, adding a bench and other architectural features to make it a woodland wild garden. More manipulation will be nec-essary in a younger woods, thick with saplings, or under shade trees growing in a lawn, but the resulting look can be the same.

The woodland wild garden is more than just a pretty face. It reaches out to the environment beyond the perimeter of the yard. Through the use of indigenous plants, common or rare, it becomes a link in a chain of life that began long before European settlement of the region.

Even the smallest wildflower nourishes or shelters animals or insects which, in turn, support larger creatures in the food web. Each is vital to a healthy ecosystem that makes up the world beyond the cul-de-sac and shopping mall.

A Midwestern woodland garden rebels against homogenization and the assembly-line approach to landscaping. It embraces the unique plants and native communities in your own neighborhood, instead of the junipers, honeylocusts, and other all-too-familiar plants used similarly in landscapes across the country. It battles against the conquest of alien species such as Norway maples and buckthorn, ambitious spreaders that move from garden sites into wild areas, forcing out our natives.

Local native plants such as witch hazels, wood anemones, pagoda dogwoods, and hop hornbeams can be found thriving in the native soil despite the worst winters and latest spring freezes your area can offer. They persist without fertilizer, pesticides, or fungicides and can continue to do so if grown in conditions to which they are naturally suited.

Landscape designers who specialize in woodland wild gardens often allow nature to have a ruling hand in the garden. Designers set the stage—using appropriate shade trees and wind barriers, selecting harmonious communities of plants, interjecting paths for

Maidenhair fern, a less common Midwestern woodland plant, has intricate and dainty green fronds.

A gravel walk cuts through a wild garden of foamflower and wild geranium.

design strength and access—and then allow the native plants to grow as they will. In this role, the designer serves as advisor and guide while the plants themselves create the garden dynamics.

Goldthread is a woodland wildflower that has been used as a fabric dye.

In this chapter, you'll learn how several landscape designers approach their work. One of them, Cliff Miller, uses older native trees to read the landscape, to learn about its original character, and to re-create woodland scenes. Brian Parsons, native plant consultant and designer of the wildflower garden at Holden Arboretum in Kirtland, Ohio, has included many of the typical plant communities of Ohio in one singularly beautiful garden. Pat Armstrong, a designer with her own renowned prairie garden and woodland wildflower garden, is active with Wild Ones, a group that promotes the use of native plants.

Re-creating Native Woodlands

Where cities and subdivisions have spread, it can be hard to imagine what kinds of native flora once occupied the land. But there are living monuments, trees that colonized the area before European settlement, that help piece together the past.

"Trees don't lie. They are the oldest living things left in any given place," says Cliff Miller, a registered landscape architect who lives in Lake Forest, Illinois, and works out of Lake Bluff.

Lake Forest still has some of its original bur oaks and swamp white oaks, which indicate that the land where lawns and parks now grow was once oaken woodlands and savannas on heavy clay subsoils. Because these oaks leaf out late in spring, woodland wildflowers would have been rich and abundant, with a long window of sunlight to nourish their growth.

Piecing together the past to provide ideas for modern designs uses a process Miller calls ecomodeling. It is a common-sense

Opposite: In spring, foamflower, wild geranium, and naturalized woodland forget-me-not make a harmonious combination.

Wild hyacinths thrive in moist areas and often are found near rivers and streams.

approach, putting plants where they are ideally suited and where they would grow if arising spontaneously in nature.

"Every plant came from somewhere," Miller says. "Find a site that is similar to your yard and use the plants that grow naturally there. People get into trouble when they forget this simple concept. Interplanting Scotch pines, which need well-drained soil, for instance, with red-twig dogwoods, which love wet, low-lying sites, is a mixture that is doomed from the start."

A striking example of ecomodeling is found at a large upscale property and naturalized landscape that Miller designed and installed in 1995. The twenty-four-acre tract includes a spreading lawn, large backyard patio, stable, and pond, with more formal foundation plantings and perennial gardens located near the house. Large, mature oaks and hickories grow in open groves across the property, with a wildflower-festooned lawn spreading beneath them.

The ordinary bluegrass and fescue lawn shelters prairie natives such as prairie trillium, with handsome maroon-mottled leaves and maroon flowers; golden star grass; and shooting-stars with back-swept pink or white petals that resemble the flaming tails of shooting stars. The landscape also includes pussy-toes, with their silvery leaves and furry flower buds, and spring-beauties, petite white flowers found in many Midwestern woods. Because the lawn had never been treated with herbicides, many of the unusual wildflowers have survived in the lawn naturally.

🪶

"Early settlers of Ohio were greeted by expansive forests, wetlands, and prairies. Adapting this wilderness to farmland forever changed the face of Ohio's landscape. Almost every mature tree had been cut by 1900; forests which formerly covered 95 percent of the state now cover only 25 percent."

—MYRTLE S. HOLDEN WILDFLOWER GARDEN, A HISTORY, HOLDEN ARBORETUM AND BRIAN PARSONS

To encourage even more color, Miller has overseeded the yard with Virginia bluebells, wild anemones, wild geraniums, forget-me-nots, and other woodland flowers able to grow amid the grass.

The lawn has become a link to natural areas surrounding the home. On one side is a rare black-soil prairie preserve; on the other is an oak-hickory woods. The landscaping, the home, and its occupants have become connected with the site and with the life all around.

Woodland re-creations, for all their ecological advantages, are still gardens and should enhance the home as well as the surroundings, Miller says. He often designs landscapes that change from more cultivated gardens near the house to wilder areas beyond. One way to accomplish this is to shift from the use of highly uniform, long-flowering, German-bred 'Goldstrum' golden coneflowers, for instance, to native black-eyed Susans. In the foundation planting of rhododendrons and pachysandra he also includes natives such as

Shooting-star, with handsome backswept petals, can grow in lightly shaded lawns.

Virginia bluebells also thrive in a shady lawn.

witch hazel, Pennsylvania sedge, and Virginia creeper. In perennial borders of 'Palace Purple' coralbells and 'Sunny Border Blue' veronica, he mixes in native prairie dropseed grass.

"I try to make a home be a home and a natural setting be harmonious with the real landscape," Miller says.

Miller finds inspiration in the work of early-twentieth-century landscape designer Jens Jensen, who designed dynamic native Midwestern landscapes but, unfortunately, didn't allow for the effects of succession. Just as old fields turn into woods with time, Jensen's wild areas have evolved into different, more mature ecosystems, leaving few good examples of his work. However, while most of Jensen's landscapes have disappeared, the concepts remain viable.

"They didn't understand the dynamics of ecology then. They thought they could leave the plantings alone and they would stay the same. We now know that you have to manage them—for example, by applying fires to prairies to mimic the forces that created the ecosystem," Miller says.

CREATING THE RIGHT HABITAT

Ecomodeling is essential for growing the white birch or paper birch, which often fail in many Midwestern landscapes due to the destructive bronze birch borer. The borer attacks when the plants, which prefer northern habitats, become stressed by hot and dry weather.

The trick, says Cliff Miller, is to plant white birches in soil that is simultaneously moist and well-aerated, a combination hard to achieve in ordinary soil. He suggests amending the planting site with gravel backfill. Use 1-inch-diameter, river-washed gravel contained in a geotextile fabric and connect it to a subsurface drainage system. This simulates the moist soil and fast water drainage found beside a gravel-bedded stream, a typical habitat for the trees. The trees probably will also need an annual stem treatment for borers.

Looking at the Big Picture

Well-known for his naturalistic gardens and land-scapes, Cliff Miller is not a designer to be pigeon-holed. With his design/build firm, P. Clifford Miller, Inc., he has produced landscapes ranging from hand-some vegetable and herb gardens to perennial gardens to vegetation-filtered water gardens.

Like many other Midwestern designers, Miller can trace his interest in the landscape back to child-hood. As a boy, he liked to catch toads, salamanders, and snakes and kept them in landscaped terrariums so they would feel at home.

With a formal training in sculpture and an early career as an environmental education teacher for the Cook County Forest Preserve District, Miller found landscape design to be a logical calling.

"When I'm out in the field, I think less about the two-dimensional details as they would be drawn on a blueprint and more about a third dimension—accessing the sculptural form of the house and property," Miller says.

When he was twenty-five years old, Miller decided sculpting and teaching couldn't hold his interest and returned to landscaping, in which he had labored in high school and college. He worked briefly for two design/build firms, finding fault in both. What he needed was a company that suited his own style—so he formed his own design firm.

Miller makes preliminary plans on paper, but does most of the fine-tuning in the field. The two-dimensional blueprint provides basic positioning and plant numbers, but Miller manipulates the final placement and planting details on the land itself, saying that this brings the design process to a higher plane of perfection.

As often as he can, Miller retreats to his cabin on 160 acres in rural Michigan to recharge his creative batteries, drink in nature, and have time to philosophize and brainstorm. This allows him to return to his thriving design practice with a fresh and innovative outlook.

Landscape architect Cliff Miller believes best results come from putting landscape plants in sites similar to their native habitats.

COMBINING NATIVE AND CULTIVATED PLANTS

Native plants need not be isolated in their own separate space but can make handsome ground-covering blends with certain cultivated plants. Instead of underplanting shrubs, trees, and other partly sunny or shady gardens with ivy or pachysandra, Cliff Miller makes a matrix of native and cultivated perennials.

His formula blend grows into a dense, attractive, and low-maintenance ground cover, a new dimension in design. Plants used in the matrix include the following. Those marked with an asterisk are Midwestern natives.

- Big-leaved aster *
- Shooting-star *
- Common oak sedge *
- Broad-leaved goldenrod *
- Wild geranium *
- Woodland phlox *
- Wild ginger *
- 'Metallica Crispa' pyramidal bugleweed
- Chinese forget-me-not
- Epimedium
- Red barrenwort
- 'Blue Dart' periwinkle
- Lady's-mantle

In his free time (of which there is little), Miller writes essays and poetry about the Midwest.

A Varied Habitat Woodland Garden

Woodland plants change with the terrain and the resources the land offers. Woodland plants find the balance of moisture, soil, and space that suits them best, drifting into alliances with other plants that have similar needs and forming unique communities. In the moist floodplain beside a creek, you might find black walnuts, sycamores, and marsh marigolds while an upland slope may harbor hickories, white oaks, and false Solomon's-seal.

The Holden Arboretum Myrtle S. Holden Wildflower Garden, designed by Brian Parsons, compresses a variety of woodland habitats into one large garden that glows with color in spring. The five-acre garden, which includes a prairie and bog area and a limestone and sandstone rockery, is home to 700 species of native plants.

The wildflower garden originated in 1968 as a way to showcase flora from the 3,100-acre arboretum grounds. The original garden contained only plants found at the arboretum but grew as arboretum volunteers ventured deeper into the woodlands, returning with more plants for the garden.

Starry false Solomon's-seal grows beside wild hyacinth.

"It is a way to focus on what is best about the area," Parsons says.

As the garden took shape beneath an oak and maple grove, its goal was expanded to include species from across Ohio and also a few federally threatened, endangered, or proposed threatened species from outside Ohio.

At that point, Parsons stepped in to take charge. He opted to divide the garden into different plant communities—an upland area with hemlocks and white pines, a creek area, a fern garden,

A community of wild geraniums, woodland phlox, and miterwort display contrasting foliage and form.

PARSONS' SOIL RECIPES

For a neutral-soil wildflower mix, blend 2 parts neutral leaf mold, 1 part existing topsoil, 1 part riverbank gravel or coarse grit, and 1 part well-rotted wood chips.

For wildflowers needing acidic soil, blend 1 part Canadian peat moss or well-rotted oak leaf mold and 1 part silica sand.

To each, add an inch or two of partly rotted leaves and wood chips each year to keep the soil rich in organic matter.

Opposite: At one entrance to the Holden Arboretum Wildflower Garden, there is a rockery for native plants.

and a wooded glade. Parsons carved an exaggerated slope into a hillside, making conditions suitable for each type of community. He bolstered the garden's design by adding winding paths that divide different sections of the garden and draw the eye throughout. They are all topped with washed riverbank gravel, all of the same color and consistency for design unity.

"This has developed like a jigsaw puzzle. I had an image of the finished garden but have had to put all the different pieces in place to achieve it," Parsons says.

Beyond the ecological implications, these different habitats allow Parsons to squeeze in as many blooming plants as possible, making a striking spring display.

In the floodplain area, along a small creek, the soil is rich with moisture and silt deposited by occasional flooding. It is a beautiful but naturally transient community based on the whims of spring rainfall and flooding. Various species thrive there—lily-leaved white hellebore, ostrich fern, bee balm, Canada lily, blue iris, spicebush, pawpaw trees, a rare

Nearby are other uncommon habitats for Ohio natives like the hardy prickly pear cactus.

Aggressive but beautiful golden ragwort thrives in the young floodplain garden.

pumpkin ash, butternut walnut, and pagoda dogwood. Golden ragwort, an aggressive spreading wildflower with golden June flowers, covers every open space.

"Golden ragwort may be too abundant but leaves no openings for weeds," Parsons says. "It also is appropriate for the young stage of this floodplain and will be squeezed out as the area matures and other plants come in. It helps to know what stage in the evolution of the area certain species arrive so that you don't introduce them too early or too late."

The garden's Pierson Creek ravine area has flora typical of moist ravine bottoms in northeast Ohio. Nestled deep within dramatic ravines, the Pierson Creek area tends to stay cool and moist and harbors some of the most stunning Ohio wildflowers. There are shrubby leatherwoods, spicebushes, and witch hazels, which reveal spidery yellow flowers in fall after the autumn leaves drop. Among the smaller plants are blue cohosh, with leaves that arise blue-purple then change to green; foamflower, with handsome maple-shaped leaves and foamy spikes of white flowers; flowering raspberry, a pink-flowered vine capable of controlling erosion on a bank; and green-and-gold, a long-blooming golden-flowered ground cover. Three plants favored as medicinal herbs—goldenseal, yellow mandarin, and ginseng—also grow here.

While the peak of bloom for the rest of the garden is April to June, the fern garden comes on strong afterward. Clusters of evergreen Christmas fern blend with deciduous silver glade fern, lady fern, narrow-leaved glade fern, marginal and intermediate wood fern, spinulose wood fern, and ostrich fern, all with distinctive and handsome clusters of fronds. Although not an easy fern to cultivate, maidenhair fern makes a striking addition to the mix, with flat, rounded fronds whorling on circular stems.

The ferns rub elbows with wildflowers chosen primarily for their summer fruit—bristly podded wood poppies; doll's-eyes, with white berries that have a single dark spot and seem to be molded of porcelain; yellow mandarin, with its orange football fruit; and ginseng, with its red berries.

Near the top of the slope in a grove forested with hemlocks and yellow birch is an acidic upland community. Sugar maples typical of other gardens must be culled from this area as their autumn leaves fall in dense layers that would smother the more petite wildflowers. Here you'll find Canada mayflower, interrupted fern, robin-runaway, wintergreen, Oconee-bells, and galax.

Making Transitions

Brian Parsons, on the staff of Holden Arboretum for over twenty years, is a hands-on horticulturist and naturalist. A coastal Maine resident who dreamed of working in oceanography, he shifted his life course while attending college in the landlocked Midwest. While studying classics, he took a few botany classes that included field trips to the Morton Arboretum in Lisle, Illinois. There he learned about native plants, plant communities, species relationships, and succession. Intrigued, he accepted an internship at Holden Arboretum after graduating and has been there ever since.

Parsons served as the arboretum's assistant superintendent of grounds but after dabbling in botanical field exploration with infectiously enthusiastic botanists Jim Bissell and Tom Yates, he took over as the arboretum's field naturalist. Now, as natural areas coordinator, he oversees the wildflower garden and many more acres of wild lands in the arboretum holdings.

Working as a consultant, Parsons encourages native-plant

At Holden Arboretum, Brian Parsons has created one of the finest Midwestern wildflower gardens.

Fire pinks mix with purple-leaf coralbells and woodland poppies in a transitional garden.

gardeners to analyze a site thoroughly before planning and planting. Look for problem areas that can be solved with site work or design, he says. Incorporate the relationship of the house to the property so you can make a compatible mix with the garden. Analyze where utility lines will go. Water access is particularly important, he cautions. If not irrigated in summer, woodland garden greenery will fall dormant and the garden will lose some of its appeal. Play up unique features like natural rock formations or streams. Work within the constraints of the natural soil type, for a garden will grow most easily where it is naturally adapted.

Parsons believes in including a diversity of plants, both for interest and for environmental impact. Whenever possible, he will repeat a few attractive and widely adapted plants for a sense of rhythm. Ground covers like green-and-gold, woodland poppies, ferns, and dwarf crested irises are good minglers that help to unify gardens representing different woodland settings.

His gardens flow across the property, making gradual transitions from wild to tame parts of the yard. Cultivated natives such as fire pink, purple-leaved coralbells, 'Beehive' dwarf Canada hemlock, 'Spring Delight' phlox, sumacs, bee balms, beardtongues, columbines, and red-leaf 'Forest Pansy' redbuds serve this purpose well.

A Woodland Retreat

A woodland garden need not be large to be appreciated. In a shady nook beneath a single bur oak tree, landscape designer Pat Armstrong has created a dynamic garden of native plants. It complements the prairie garden that occupies the remainder of her suburban yard in Naperville, Illinois.

In 1983, Armstrong bought the lot, built a passive-solar-heated home, and began preparations for her woodland garden. She put snow fencing in the 20-foot-wide side yard below the tree and filled it with a layer of bark chips 6 inches deep. The chips smothered the weedy quackgrass below and decayed to make a fertile soil layer for woodland flowers.

Unusual white-flowered Virginia bluebells bloom behind the bold umbrella-shaped leaves of mayapples.

Dutchman's-breeches have colonized a stone retaining wall.

To screen off the woodland garden from the street, Armstrong planted a shrubby barrier of arrowwood viburnum and pagoda dogwoods. The birds further assisted this process by sowing red- and yellow-twig dogwoods amid the informal hedge. A stone retaining wall sprouting Dutchman's-breeches and columbines is inset into the slope near the house to make a dynamic structural feature. An unobtrusive stepping-stone walk parallels the stone wall, allowing visitors to walk in the garden without treading on emerging flowers.

The first wildflowers were transplants from the house where Armstrong previously lived. Others came from seeds collected at Morton Arboretum and in southern Wisconsin.

"I just squished them into the wood chips the first spring and fall of the garden, and they came up by themselves," Armstrong says.

Although often slower to put on a show than wildflowers grown from cuttings or divisions, seed-started wildflowers represent a broad spectrum of genetic characteristics and help expand the adaptability of the species.

False rue anemone flowers in enough profusion to enjoy from afar.

Large-flowered bellworts bear striking yellow flowers.

Flowers are allowed to arise and spread where they will, as in a natural ecosystem. They mingle amid the tree roots and creep beside the walk.

Even without human manipulation, some beautiful combinations develop. Woodland poppies, with bright open-faced yellow flowers, complement the dangling blue flowers of Virginia bluebells. False rue anemone spreads into a ground-covering sweep of fine foliage and small but abundant white flowers. Its namesake, the rue anemone, appears in smaller clumps scattered here and there. The early May garden has the rhythm of these repeated blue, white, and yellow flowers, plus a sprinkling of other flowers for spice.

Great white trillium, once an abundant spring flower now threatened by deer browsing in many areas, thrives here. Red prairie trillium shows off handsome mottled foliage and small flowers with back-bending petals. Pretty bellworts arise in upright

Pat Armstrong is a native-plant proponent who practices what she preaches in her suburban yard.

clumps, suspending yellow, bell-shaped flowers, a pleasant contrast to open-faced anemones and poppies.

Later in spring, wild geraniums and phacelia, collected from southern Illinois, re-create the garden dynamics, along with ferns, Solomon's-seal, and Solomon's-plumes. Summer and fall feature goldenrods, woodland asters, Joe-Pye weed, and white-flowered anise hyssop, which thrive in the perimeter areas lit by morning and late afternoon sun.

Summer flowers are complemented by red and blue berries of Solomon's seal and Solomon's plume and green calyx stars of orange horse gentian. Jewelweed offers yellow and orange flowers in summer and handsome yellow foliage in fall.

From these modest beginnings, a teeming wildflower garden has arisen. Its only maintenance need is a layer of autumn leaves that decay and enrich the soil.

Native Know-how

Pat Armstrong is a woman of many talents—a botanist and ecologist, former biology teacher, and former manager of the Schulenberg Prairie at the Morton Arboretum.

"I've been interested in nature since I was a toddler. I caught critters—frogs, minnows, crayfish, turtles—and tried to provide a place for them to live. This meant creating habitats with plants, water, and the things they like to eat. I spent hours in the woods, picking and eating berries, and when I got tired of that, I looked at the plants," Armstrong says. "I still like to do that today!"

A Michigan native, Armstrong moved west of Chicago in 1954 and has stayed there ever since. In addition to having master's degrees in botany and ecology, Armstrong likes to paint and photograph plants and flowers and is given rich opportunities for both in her own back yard.

Throughout her career, Armstrong has been bombarded with questions about native gardening. In 1985, she went into business for herself, doing native planting consultation and design. She travels to Iowa, Michigan, Wisconsin, and to other sites in Illinois, providing ideas and information.

AGGRESSIVE NON-NATIVES TO AVOID

Some commonly planted landscape plants are aggressive spreaders, likely to escape and overrun wild areas. Avoid planting species such as the following, Pat Armstrong advises.

Norway maple	Japanese honeysuckle
White mulberry	Buckthorn
White poplar	Multiflora rose
Black locust	Oriental bittersweet
Siberian elm	Winter creeper
Japanese barberry	Lily-of-the-valley
Amur honeysuckle	Moneywort
Morrow's honeysuckle	Mexican bamboo
Tartarian honeysuckle	Periwinkle or myrtle

While Armstrong prefers to work with strictly native plants, she advises her clients to consider what they want from their gardens before planting.

"Set ground rules and goals so you are clear on what you want to accomplish," she says. "Then you won't be swayed by spur-of-the-moment whims that will distract you."

Armstrong, along with Vicki Nowicki (see page 197), is one of the founders of the Chicago chapter of Wild Ones, a nonprofit organization devoted to natural landscaping. Armstrong also has published a series of native plant information sheets and brochures, as well as the *Wild Plant Family Cookbook*, which contains 978 recipes for wild greens, berries, and similar edibles.

Five

CONIFER HAVENS

❧

In the Midwest, where deciduous trees can be dormant for six months of the year, evergreens are an important part of any landscape. They become most prominent after autumn leaves have fallen and the rest of the landscape looks bare and brown. On a drab February day, there is nothing quite so cheerful as the long, silky needles of a white pine or the thick pyramid of a blue spruce.

Japanese maples and hostas complement a mature Colorado blue spruce at Girard Nurseries.

Evergreens are stalwart elements of a mixed border that never need dividing and, if properly selected, seldom need pruning. During the growing season their striking broad or needle-shaped leaves of green, chartreuse, smoky gray, blue-green, or silver offer textures and shapes not often seen among other plants. This makes them interesting companions for ornamental grasses, perennials, and flowering trees and shrubs.

'Globosa' Colorado blue spruce looks handsome year-round.

Common yew, juniper, arborvitae, pine, and Norway spruce are well-known in Midwestern landscapes. But these ordinary evergreens are only a fraction of what is available from a conifer specialist. Among the hundreds of unusual cultivars of evergreens, you may find a 'Pendula' limber pine, a weeping cultivar that spreads across the ground, or an 'Oculus-draconis' Japanese red pine with golden-ringed needles. 'Uncle Fogy' jack pine has bizarre weeping branches. 'Aurea' mugo pine turns golden in winter, while 'Blue Wave' Japanese white pine is turquoise with undulating branches.

Choosing among these unusual varieties can become habit-forming. It has, in fact, shaped the worlds of nurserymen Jeff Forinash of Girard Nurseries in Geneva, Ohio, and Rich Eyre of Rich's Foxwillow Pines Nursery in Woodstock, Illinois, who have devoted their lives to propagating, growing, and designing with conifers. This chapter is dedicated to plant combinations and design ideas from their display gardens.

A Coniferous Foliage Garden

While some nurseries have small display gardens of annuals or perennials, Girard Nurseries goes above and beyond, with five acres of conifer-dominated gardens. Carefully chosen for contrasting textures, sizes, shapes, and colors, the conifers are mingled with companion plants like Japanese maples, kousa dogwoods, and daylilies.

The gardens spread around nursery owner Peter Girard's house, filling the front and back yards. The collection resembles a series of island beds, with gravel or turf paths winding between them. Each bend in a path reveals handsome new scenes.

The front garden is dominated by a huge weeping European beech, with many coniferous gems nestled beneath its canopy and beyond. Another remarkable specimen, 'Acrocona' Norway spruce, is one of the first trees visitors notice. It sends out exotic purple-red flowers in spring, a brilliant display. Treated as a specimen of distinction, it stands out in a bed of its own near a bench carved with comical bears.

Across a grass path, a much quieter but equally rare conifer resides behind a cluster of 'Stella de Oro' daylilies. It is a dwarf

The rat tail spruce bears bristling needles at the branch ends.

'Acrocona' Norway spruce has colorful flowers and cones.

Douglas fir, which has only grown to 3 feet high in the dozen years Jeff Forinash has grown it.

Farther down the walk is 'Silberlocke', a silver-colored fir with curled needles that display their frosted undersides. It is grown in a raised bed of well-drained loam, which firs find to be ideal.

The path takes a turn, and suddenly a wide waterfall, enveloped in evergreens, unfolds above a pond. Ground-hugging weeping limber pine spreads along the flat surface on each side of the pond. The trickling waterfall is framed on both sides by a lay-

'Silberlocke' displays silver-colored needles that appear to be frosted by snow.

ered sequence of low, mounded 'Hillside Creeper' Scotch pines, dramatic weeping 'Pendula' white pines, and 'Sargentii' weeping hemlocks.

The needled conifers form striking contrast to the large blue leaves of *Hosta sieboldiana*, the glossy green leaves of *Hosta montana*, and red-leaved Japanese maples such as 'Skeeter's Broom' and 'Crimson Queen'. Throughout the garden, rhododendrons and azaleas mingle, providing spring flowers and contrast in leaf form.

"When using color, I like to mix it up so the garden won't become monotonous," Forinash says. "Instead of blending several different shades of yellow, I mix yellow with green, and it looks that much brighter."

A small creek makes an interesting place for a naturalistic garden.

'St. Mary's Broom' blue spruce makes a dynamic color contrast with red dianthus.

That colorful approach is evident farther down the path, where a bridge crosses a winding creek. Once a weed-filled eyesore, now the creek banks are clad in contorted filberts; kousa dogwoods such as 'Weaver's Weeping', 'Lustgarten Weeping', and variegated 'Gold Star'; daylilies; astilbe; and aggressive, slope-holding variegated grass.

High and dry in the upland beyond, the display of varied evergreens continues. The walk curves around yet another clump of greenery, suddenly surprising the visitor with a large, formal fountain. Nearby grow tropical-looking umbrella pines, with whorled needles that splay at the ends of branches. Both the green-leaved and rare 'Osario Gold' forms grow well here near Lake Erie, where protective winter snows are deep.

The backyard garden features a similar blend of walkways, dynamic views, focal points, and interesting conifers. A 40-foot-wide lawn opening leads to a cedar and redwood gazebo, a common haven for wedding photos and even high school graduations.

Whimsical statuary adds interest to the grounds. The collection includes a ghostly white carousel horse of authentic size, a Victorian street light, and Nebraskan farm art—recycled pieces of garden tools welded into shovel turkeys and other ingenious designs by winter-bound Nebraskan ranchers.

Umbrella pines have a tropical look.

Above: This gazebo has become a place for community gatherings.

Left: A formal fountain is surrounded by ornamental grasses and conifers.

Right: A weeping larch cascades beside a dwarf linden.

Below: Golden-needled 'Natural Life' golden white pine is combined with a kousa dogwood.

There are many charming combinations throughout the gardens, including 'Natural Life' golden white pine with red-leaved Japanese maple. 'Little Bunny', a tiny tufted form of fountain grass, looks handsome in the foreground of 'Skylands' yellow-needled Oriental golden spruce. 'Maxwellii', a miniature, mounded form of Norway spruce, can make an interesting foreground planting for 'Natural Life' golden white pine and kousa dogwood. The twisting limbs of 'Uncle Fogy' jack pine contrast nicely with 'Lutea', a golden-leaved form of Hinoki cypress. In mild winter areas, try 'Osario Gold' umbrella pine with the fine-needled, shrubby, deciduous evergreen 'Lanark' European larch.

'Sargentii' weeping hemlocks mix with mountain ashes, and 'Hornibrookiana' dwarf Austrian pine combines with 'Pendula' weeping bald cypress. For marvelous color, there is purple-leaf weeping European beech with 'Prostrata' blue noble fir, and 'Pell Lake', a prostrate Norway spruce, with green 'Waterfall' Japanese maple.

The ideas for plant and color combinations, introductions to new conifers and their perennial and deciduous

The form of a weeping Norway spruce is always eye catching.

companions, and intriguing ways to create island beds, walks, and privacy screens come nonstop along every walk. They prove that a garden of conifers can be just as joyous as any other, but their impact will last even longer.

Versatility Is the Key

Jeff Forinash of Girard Nurseries designs and installs conifer-driven landscapes. Girard, one of the best sources for unusual conifers in the Midwest, can supply both plants and a landscape design for its customers.

Jeff Forinash, a Girard Nurseries landscape specialist, stands to the left of nursery owner Peter Girard.

'Dwarf Yellow Tipped' hemlocks make a naturally low hedge suitable for light shade.

Opposite: 'Skyland' Oriental golden spruce is underplanted with 'Little Bunny' fountain grass.

Forinash lives and breathes conifers, and his entire family is involved in the nursery. His wife, Roberta, is the office manager and daughter of nursery owner Peter Girard, while his two teenage sons do odd jobs around the property. Because the nursery and landscape division are small and family-operated, Forinash wears many hats, handling the plumbing, plant propagating, and landscaping.

"You can get a wide range of effects using conifers—much more than just the ordinary row of clipped yews. You can make a very natural privacy screen or waterside planting using layers of prostrate conifers up to tall trees and interesting combinations of

textures," Forinash says. "Making these kinds of blends can soften a yard, create nice, quiet areas—plus, of course, give you a variety of ways to show off the plants."

Forinash recommends looking for dwarf and colored-leaf varieties of pines, hemlocks, and spruces for small gardens, the front of garden beds, or foundation plantings. You can also find varying leaf and tree forms, from 'Whip' Canada hemlock, with open branching and needles so short they seem artificial, to the open plumes of the rat tail spruce.

Among the best companion plants, says Forinash, are hostas and astilbes for shade (where most golden-leaved conifers are most at home). Daylilies, red-leaved Japanese maples, kousa dogwoods, and witch hazels excel in sun.

A Conifer Collector's Garden

Rich Eyre of Rich's Foxwillow Pines Nursery is a collector-turned-nurseryman with more than 2,000 varieties of interesting conifers and 1,000 varieties of woody companion plants. He grows them in a six-acre arboretum and nursery with special display gardens blended around rocks, water, and, most interesting, a red brick patio of blue spruces.

"I'm here to radicalize the gardening public—to let them know that there is

'Stella de Oro' daylily provides a long season of color beside this dwarf Douglas fir.

more to the garden than junipers, arborvitaes, and yews," he says. "The amount of fun I'm having doing it should be illegal and illicit, but thankfully it isn't. I'm pleased to be a spokesperson for my plants and a channel for the other conifer collectors who taught me."

When hosting a meeting of the National Conifer Society in 1997, Eyre massed his large collection of blue spruces into one garden of over 100 varieties. The repetition of all of these related plants provides the garden with unity and continuity while the differences in form, shape, and color provide interest.

"It's an optical treat. When they are all together, the subtleties in the species are so pronounced," Eyre says.

The spruces come predominantly in varying shades of blue and surround the large patio with undulating margins used as planting pockets. There are deep icy blue cultivars, turquoise blue cultivars, and other types that are quiet green. Standard, lollipop-shaped tree forms such as 'Globosa' Colorado spruce mix with narrow weeping 'Pendulens' Colorado spruce and upright 'Otto van Bismark'. Companion plants such as flowering onions, purple coneflowers, and yellow daylilies provide accent color.

Dozens of different Colorado spruces make up this collector's garden.

'Lutea', the golden Colorado spruce, stands out beside its blue relatives.

Man With a Mission

Rich Eyre calls himself a proponent of the American mixed perennial garden and has strong ideas on how conifers and other plants should be used in the landscape. He proposes using mixed beds to build "walls" in the yard along the most commonly used sight lines—beyond a living room picture window or a family room glass door.

He suggests creating a raised bed out of a naturalistic berm with a long, tapered slope facing the house. This will let you add many layers of plants of increasing height, a complex staging put right where you can enjoy it most. Block unwanted views with large and medium-sized conifers, then feather smaller plants down around them.

"Why give the neighbor across the street the best plants to see?" Eyre writes in one of his catalogues.

Use interesting weeping evergreens, creeping junipers, and other colorful or dwarf conifers to make the framework for the garden, putting the tallest toward the rear and the lowest in the front. Narrow, upright plants are particularly useful, Eyre says, because they provide height and take up only a modest amount of space.

Eyre also believes in using boulders, a primal element in any garden, in naturalistic clusters for more structure and staging support. Dig them into the ground for a natural look.

"A good rock is worth three trees," Eyre says.

Blend a creative mix of colors, textures, shapes, and forms, avoiding too much repetition of similar plants. For best growing success, place more tender plants on the north side of a slope or larger evergreen, so they will escape damaging winter sun and will delay growing until mid-spring, when temperatures become more moderate.

"I call this kind of landscaping enviroart. It is my passion and art form," Eyre says.

Six

MIXED GARDENS

ost landscapes include a mixture of woody and herbaceous plants, flowers, and grasses. Woody plants contribute to the traditional bones, lines, enclosures, height, and scale of the garden while the herbaceous plants are the transient and ephemeral fillers.

In the mixed border, categorizing and separating different types of plants is abolished; the mix is made freely and the results are exciting. Woody

Willow-leaved amsonia, 'Royal Cloak' barberry, and 'Ile de France' butterfly bush mix with lilies, daylilies, and bear's-breech in Craig Bergmann's mixed garden.

Climbing hydrangea is graceful even when fading out of flower.

trees and shrubs form the tallest tier and provide stability for smaller elements in vegetation-dense gardens. Herbaceous flowers, ground covers, and vines blend together to create one dynamic image of splendid complexity.

"Mixed borders hold more kinds of plants than are commonly seen in our gardens. The resulting variety of plant habit, form, and size continually refreshes the eye and creates more stimulating pictures than the usual breadloaf topography of the herbaceous border," Ann Lovejoy wrote in *Horticulture* magazine in January 1991.

Espaliered fruit trees, their arms arranged in crossing, upright, fan-shaped, or angular patterns, climb on brick walls. Vines—climbing hydrangeas, wisteria, trumpet creeper, or runner beans—twine up tree trunks and around posts, poles, and pillars. Evergreens form foliar duets with colored-leaved perennials, and annuals fill in gaps, keeping the garden full and flowing.

Mixed gardens may appear in the form of traditional borders—rectangular gardens set against the backdrop of a hedge or fence. They may serve as island beds, enveloped in lawn and planned for viewing from all sides. They may be set near a patio, nestled against the house like a foundation planting, or run along the driveway or garden path. With a mixed border, anything goes.

Plants well suited for mixed borders are generally attractive in leaf, flower, and fruit and can include woody plants like roses, hydrangeas, barberries, and Japanese maples. A key consideration is that the plants should not be aggressive spreaders or overly greedy rooters. Other good candidates are most perennials (as long as they don't spread too rampantly), many annuals, herbs, and even vegetables.

When it comes to designing mixed gardens, one of the best design teams in the Midwest is Craig Bergmann and James Grigsby, of Craig Bergmann Landscape Design, Inc., of Wilmette, Illinois. This chapter takes a look at three of their gardens—a large estate garden, a suburban home garden, and their own small urban cottage garden.

Intricate Elegance Is Their Motto

Craig Bergmann and James Grigsby are a well-matched team running one of the finest landscape architectural and design firms in the Chicago area. They design gardens all over the country and install and maintain landscapes within a thirty-mile radius of their base in Wilmette.

The duo began collaborating about sixteen years ago, when Bergmann, a newly graduated biology student with a minor in botany, was managing a florist shop. Although untrained in floral design, his creative cut-flower work drew the notice of a Chicago-area woman who was considering installing a new flower garden. She asked Bergmann to design it as a birthday present for her husband.

The stunning garden, completed with Grigsby's assistance, created a stir among others in the area. Before long, Bergmann and Grigsby had enough work to enter the landscape design field full time.

Part of Bergmann's success is due to his enthusiasm for plants and his interest in trying new species, blending intriguing combinations, and playing with color. He has an almost photographic memory and good sense of space, so he can capture new ideas from gardens he sees anywhere.

Craig Bergmann often takes Forest, his Tibetan terrier, on the job.

At Craig Bergmann's Country Garden, a garden center, a Belgian fence espalier is made of apple trees.

Although now he is a landscape architect registered in Illinois, Bergmann is glad that he learned the profession through working with plants rather than on the drafting board.

Grigsby, Bergmann's alter ego, is a former professor at The Art Institute of Chicago. He focuses his talents on the business end of the company and serves as a creative consultant, giving a fresh perspective on questions of color, texture, and proportion.

"These elements are so important if you want a garden to look like it belongs to the property," Grigsby says. "You need to give it a sense of place, and it takes special thought to make that happen."

Bergmann's gardens are so innovative and complex that the duo quickly discovered that not just anybody could maintain them.

"We were seduced into starting our own after-care division so that we could be certain that trained gardeners were keeping the properties in top condition," Grigsby says.

Each gardener they hire has a horticultural background and spends two years working as an apprentice with experienced crew members. The gardeners must know cultivated plants from weeds and what tasks need to be done at any given time. They also must have an artistic sense, being able to stake plants so they look like they appeared from spilled seeds or to prune shrubs so they are natural but controlled.

Because Bergmann draws on a palette of nearly 2,000 herbaceous plants—many of which are not commonly available—he started Craig Bergmann's Country Garden, a perennial nursery and garden center in Winthrop Harbor, Illinois. Providing his own plants allows the company access to top-quality plants any time they are needed.

"The Country Garden is a true garden center, in the European sense of the word. We don't sell anything we don't use ourselves," Grigsby says.

Display gardens at the nursery give customers new ideas for their own yards. A Belgian espalier, with angled branches forming diamond-shaped openings in a living fence, surrounds a circular rose and herb garden.

A woodland walk, with steps made from slices of tree trunks, passes beside dogwoods, Scotch pines, hawthorns, sweet woodruff, 'Lilafee' epimedium, Chinese forget-me-not, summer snowflakes, yellow wood poppy, Virginia bluebells, and yellow primroses.

A new Autumn Garden, with plants that peak as the growing season ebbs, has just been completed.

Although Bergmann's is one of the most popular design firms in Chicago, he limits the number of new clients he will take on. He insists on being personally involved in every design job, preferring to get his hands dirty in the soil rather than on carbon paper.

A Cottage Garden in the City

The small, walled space between Bergmann's early-twentieth-century farmhouse and design studio in Wilmette, Illinois, is a garden playground and masterpiece for Bergmann and Grigsby. Beds flanking each wall ripple with a variety of color themes and interesting plants seldom seen in the Midwest. The colors include bright and bold scarlets, chartreuses, and purples as well as the softer colors the duo's clients often prefer.

Beyond color orchestration, the garden is designed for year-round beauty. In spring it glows with tulips, azaleas, wildflowers, and magnolias. In summer, perennials and foliage dominate, while charming specimen plants—including rosemary and tropical begonias—catch the eye in statuesque pots.

"We want our plants to work hard, having interesting flowers and foliage at the same time," Grigsby says.

The garden entrance is an arbor-covered gate near the garage, where pots of evergreen topiary stand in a formal salute of wel-

Above: 'Menton' tulips mix with 'Antique Shades' pansies in the Apricot Garden.
Below: Complex and beautiful color schemes include such plants as 'Black Beauty' lily, 'Black Knight' delphinium, and 'Mont Blanc' lily.

come. In summer, guests are greeted by large pots of fuchsia clustered at the entrance to a small, elegant greenhouse where Bergmann and Grigsby keep their collection of rare tropicals.

To the right, a small brick path leads past a mixed border to a pergola covered with pink-flowered honeysuckle. The border features variegated plants and flowers of soft blues, pinks, and white including fallopia, weigela, rugosa roses, catmint, pink and blue larkspur, white Oriental lilies, and white spikes of black snakeroot.

To the left, the main walk lies in the shadow of a large saucer magnolia, the sole original plant on the grounds when the garden was begun. It also is one of the largest saucer magnolias north of

A walk leads from the Silver Garden toward the garden entrance.

Chicago. Grigsby attributes its size to the protection of the sheltered courtyard and careful thinning to keep the limbs from breaking under heavy snow or ice. Beneath its limbs grow an intriguing diversity of pink and blue flowers—wood phlox, Virginia bluebells, pink and purple tulips, bleeding heart, hellebores, and a blue-leaved hosta. Silver-colored Japanese painted fern, variegated Solomon's seal, glossy-leaved European ginger, and silver-spotted lungwort mix with cream-variegated euonymus and hosta.

Borders run on both sides of the main part of the garden with a small area of green lawn in the center. A narrow border called the Apricot Garden mixes a 'Golden Glory' Cornelian cherry dogwood, a hedge of 'Wintergreen' boxwood, 'Menton' tulips, roses interplanted with 'Antique Shades' pansies, chartreuse-flowered *Nicotiana langsdorffii*, English roses, and other warm-colored flowers.

Opposite: A rustic arbor and pots of fuchsia welcome visitors.

Above: Dwarf conifers cluster in pots by the gateway.

Below: Tulips, viburnums, and rhododendrons dominate the spring garden.

Clematis macropetala *twines on a porch rail above 'Oddity' hen and chicks.*

The border terminates near the house's rustic patio, where a forty-year-old standard 'Meyer' lilac is underplanted with a purple-leaf barberry, red-veined 'Sanguineus' rumex, and 'Globemaster' flowering onion. Checkerboard purple fritillarias and white pasque flowers arise through blue forget-me-nots. 'Purple Fountain' weeping European beech trees flank a stone urn.

On the opposite side of the garden, an espaliered fringe tree climbs the wall, looking like casual greenery until it bursts into bloom in late spring. A variegated porcelain vine weaves through the espalier, topping it with a fringe of white-mottled foliage. Lilies, 'Brunette' snakeroot, and heliotrope cluster before the fringe tree. Completing the scene are color-coordinated companions such as purple-flowered fritillaria, purple-leaved *Rosa glauca*, an upright red-leaf 'Royal Cloak' barberry, 'Ravenswing' chervil, 'Chameleon' euphorbia, 'Montrose Ruby' coralbells, 'Vera Jameson' sedum and, for contrast, chartreuse-flowered lady's-mantle.

In summer, the color scheme shifts slightly with the bright red blooms of 'Edith Cavell' rose, an old-fashioned polyantha. Red daylilies and crimson Asiatic lilies contrast with white flower spikes of black snakeroot. Nearby several stems of bear's-breech stand tall, with white flowers edged in purple.

Primary colors mark the shady corner near the design studio. A white-variegated elderberry swells below a white-flowered, silver-trunked shadblow tree. Red-leaved astilbes, yellow daffodils, and pastel yellow tulips mingle with Virginia bluebells near a blue-flowered hydrangea and blue-flowered clematis.

Even work areas are beautifully decorated.

This garden blends into the Silver Garden, adjacent to the crazy paving—an eye-catching mix of irregularly cut stone, brick, and glazed ceramic chards—that marks the office entrance. The garden features a dwarf blue spruce, silver-variegated lamium, 'Frosty Morn' sedum, and tender, silver-leaved lavenders. The paved area is decorated with large pots of purple- and silver-leaved rex and other begonias, with leaves so succulent and interesting they beg to be touched.

The south end of the garden, which is entered under a rustic arbor, includes a large weeping Nootka false cypress and Harry Lauder's walking stick, salvaged from a landscape renovation site where it was no longer wanted. Nearby are sweeps of epimedium; 'Carol Mackie' daphne; Aaron's-beard, with interesting yellow flowers that have ball-like tufts of stamens in the center; and a gnarly bitter orange tree, which is bundled under old Christmas trees during winter.

"The bitter orange tree is not supposed to live here, but it has for three years now. We are in 'zone denial' here. We like to stretch the limits," Grigsby says.

Under the canopy of an old 'Schwedleri' maple is a pink-flowering royal azalea, which Bergmann calls the most beautiful of the deciduous azaleas. Even though the soil is slightly alkaline, they grow easily with a mulch of pine needles and applications of acid-based fertilizer in April, May, June, and July.

Colorful echeverias make an interesting mixed container.

In a sunny opening, an arbor of stout beams is covered with 'New Dawn', a vigorous climbing rose. It is complemented by German irises, old-fashioned roses, and the tall blue spikes of delphiniums.

Even though there are hundreds of plants shoe-horned into this garden, the design flows from one section to the next. A country theme, derived from the history of the house, adds continuity with

This suburban yard has a secluded pool surrounded by mixed gardens.

elements such as trellises and handrails of rough-hewn lumber, hand-carved stone troughs, and textured stone planters.

If there is a limitation to the garden, it is sunshine. The garden receives only about four hours of sun a day, but Bergmann and his crew make the most of it. They use shade-loving plants and even sun lovers such as musk roses and *Rosa glauca* that will tolerate some shade.

What Bergmann discovers about which plants grow well here, and in the other gardens his firm tends, helps him design new landscapes in innovative ways.

"The best way to become a great gardener is to garden and learn through the trials and tribulations," confirms Grigsby.

A Suburban Sanctuary

One of Craig Bergmann's first landscape projects was the design and installation of a flower garden at a handsome suburban home. The project grew to landscaping the entire yard and upgrading the landscape scheme in following years as trees matured and children left home.

The upscale house is set sideways on a half-acre lot, which makes the landscape challenging to design. The front portion of the yard, which is visible from the street, has elements of a traditional landscape—shrub borders of yews, pines, hemlocks, and spirea. None have ever been sheared, so they retain a loose, natural shape. Flowers have not been particularly successful in this open space as deer browse on them morning, noon, and night.

Deer seldom visit the back yard, which is enclosed in a five-foot-high fence. Although deer are capable of clearing the fence, dense plantings on each side make jumping precarious. People can enter the back yard from the driveway, through an arbor-covered gate that resembles Bergmann's own.

The focal point is a large pool that takes up much of the space. Bergmann recently moved the pool equipment into a far corner, shifted the patio into a more shady area, and upgraded the patio surface from aggregate, which can snag a swimsuit if someone sits on it, to smooth flagstone set in concrete.

A stone terrace and thick mixed borders envelop the pool. The sunnier half of the garden is devoted to a pink, blue, and white color scheme including pink-flowered 'The Fairy' rose, 'Pink Delight' butterfly bushes, fragrant lavender-blue wands of lavender,

A pink-and-blue garden color scheme echoes hues in a nearby planter of 'Pink Expectation' geranium and 'Blue Wonder' fanflower.

'Butterfly Blue' pincushion flower, 'Blue Horizon' ageratums, and silvery 'Big Ears' lamb's-ears. 'Blue Wonder' fanflower and variegated Swedish ivy dangle from a nearby urn.

One difficult spot in the border seems to stay either too wet or too dry, so most plants refuse to grow there. Now it is planted with *Carex morrowii*, which seems to tolerate both extremes and blends nicely with the color scheme.

'Purple Candle' astilbe grows at the base of false spirea.

In a well-drained area, a flagstone walk slips into the garden and out a side gate, flanked with dianthus, silver thyme, and lady's-mantle. Roses, airy Russian sage, plumed pink queen-of-the-prairie, and purple globes of Brazilian verbena blend in the rear of the garden. False spirea forms a shrubby thicket with long compound leaves and, in summer, white flowers, making a handsome, spreading background. A dramatic planting of river birch with 'Ingwersen's Variety' hardy geraniums and dwarf horehounds provides an interesting combination of textures and colors at the far end of the pool.

On the shadier side of the pool, *Rosa rubrifolia* mixes with fountain grass, pink-flowered 'Cattleya' astilbe, and a patch of gooseneck loosestrife, an aggressive spreader held captive between the pool and a wall. At the back lie taller flowers such as 'Miss Lingard' early phlox, with fragrant white flowers, and *Thalictrum rochebruneanum*, a five-foot-tall meadow rue with pink flowers and pendulous yellow stamens. Catmint and 'Powis Castle' artemisia cluster near the front.

A stone path stretches from the back yard to the front through a narrow opening beside the house. Here Bergmann has re-created a New England woodland similar to the region where his client used to live. Evergreen leatherwood fern and pachysandra spread under mountain laurels, small-leaved rhododendrons, hellebores, and summer-sweet, a shade-loving shrub with spikes of fragrant white flowers in summer and fall. Since the native soil is alkaline, Bergmann amended the entire area with coarse peat moss, oak leaf

compost, and grit prior to planting. Regular use of acid-based fertilizer and Southern pine needle mulch help maintain the pH necessary for good growth.

By the backyard patio, fragrant roses mix with daylilies, and yellow snapdragons mix with cannas.

The many vignettes blended throughout this modest-sized property show that a landscape need not be large to be captivating.

An Elegant Estate

Craig Bergmann and his company also are responsible for the landscaping at a magnificent five-acre Chicago-area estate. Built by an early-twentieth-century industrialist and plant collector, it is not just a showplace. The estate is designed to tell a story—conveying the history of the property and building a sense of drama when visitors walk from the front yard to the back. The front yard is more subdued and elegant, while the privacy of the back yard is devoted to flamboyant mixed gardens.

"Every square foot has a purpose in the overall scheme, and all the plants have to be active participants, working very hard throughout the seasons," Grigsby says.

*A quiet garden in the side yard
is framed with boxwood hedges.*

When Bergmann first took on this estate garden in 1996, woody plants collected over the years were spreading randomly across the property. As a result, the landscape lacked cohesion.

Bergmann planted mixed shrub borders around the isolated woody specimens to frame the property and to focus the view. He then updated existing gardens and added a magnificent pair of perennial borders.

A simple and formal entryway with a circular drive rings a large oak tree. The central bed is rimmed with a low stone retaining wall, a compact hedge of yews, and a plush ground cover of variegated yellow archangel and variegated hebe.

A walk begins beside the house, passing to a garden of azaleas and rhododendrons that glow in spring and sit serene in summer.

The next garden along the way is a slightly more complex and formal garden. Two arching beds form an ellipse around the walk and are filled with a simple blend of perennials—variegated meadowsweet and annual mintleaf. Behind them is a formal hedge of 'Wintergreen' boxwood and more upright 'Pullman' boxwoods, named after the founder of the property. Unfortunately, 'Pullman' boxwood has not proven as hardy as 'Wintergreen' and other cold-climate boxwood selections.

A white garden, developed early in the estate's history, emerges beside the walk. It is centered on an original, black-bottomed lily pool set in a brick terrace and surrounded by a garden edged in a clipped boxwood hedge. Within this formal structure are more informal mixed gardens, blending white-flowered plants such as white foxglove and white bleeding-heart, which bloom in spring; oakleaf and 'Annabelle' hydrangeas, which bloom in summer; plus white-plumed false spirea with white-flowered Japanese anemones for fall.

The walk circles to the back yard where a bluestone terrace holds parterres of annuals. Edged in 'Green Gem' boxwood, the gardens carve geometric beds of color into the paving. In spring there is a brilliant display of red 'Oscar' tulips with blue forget-me-nots. In summer, the parterres feature red and yellow tender perennials such as 'Gartenmeister Bonstedt' fuchsias and 'Solar Flare' coleus.

A multicolored rose garden nestles beside the house, just like at an English manor house. The roses provide fragrance and cut flowers for indoor vases.

In summer all eyes are drawn to a pair of long mixed borders—65 feet long and 12 ½ feet wide—stretching in front of a 1920s yew

Above: White-variegated leaves are the common denominator among ivy, hostas, and viburnums.

Left: A lily pool is the focal point of a white garden.

A lightly shaded bed is illuminated with warm colors from 'The Line' and 'Solar Eclipse' coleus and 'Gartenmeister Bonstedt' fuchsia.

hedge. The borders lead to two new fieldstone pillars that mark the entryway into the woods beyond.

"These two borders were meant to be seen as one, and they include many similar plants, but they are not identical," says Bergmann.

Bergmann allows perennials and self-seeding annuals to find their own preferred sites, as long as they look good in the overall mix. Dignified 6-foot-high spikes of blue delphiniums appear in the rear of the borders. Along with clematis-laden tuteurs, pyramidal trellis towers, repeated along the rear of the garden, the delphiniums provide rhythm and continuity.

In mid-border, there is a blend of red, pink, blue, white, and pale yellow flowers. Easy-care roses such as pink 'Ballerina' and 'Lavender Dream' are repeated often. Large sweeps of mildew-resistant pink-flowered 'Marshall's Delight' bee balm complement pink lilies and yellow 'Moonshine' yarrow. 'Mahogany' bee balm, which needs spraying to deter mildew, stands beside annual 'Red Shield' hibiscus, which makes an ideal filler.

'Lucifer' crocosmia, a favorite of the property owners, echoes the reds of 'Gardenview Scarlet' bee balm. Red spikes of *Polygonum amplexicaule* mingle with annual Brazilian verbena; mound-shaped, lemon-yellow 'Moonbeam' coreopsis; and upright 'Blue Horizon' ageratum. 'Blue Hill' salvia mixes with pink turtlehead and white-flowered 'Tardiva' hydrangea. The garden is never stagnant. Where Oriental poppies have gone dormant, silvery stands of *Plectranthus argentatus* fill in.

This section of the long border features delphiniums, 'Mahogany' bee balm, 'Lucifer' crocosmia, and 'Yellow Tiger' lily.

A stunning yellow-and-red flower combination features 'Yellow Tiger' lily, 'Lucifer' crocosmia, and 'Gardenview Scarlet' bee balm.

The front of the border features large clusters of lady's mantle, purple-leaved 'Montrose Ruby' coralbells, 'Six Hills Giant' catmint, and 'Moonbeam' coreopsis. For ease of maintenance, the borders are edged with a bluestone mowing strip, which looks like stepping stones but holds the garden shape and allows for easy mowing. A low brick curb elevates the garden several inches above the surrounding soil, allowing for addition of extra organic matter while keeping grass roots out. The rear of the border is separated from the yew hedge with a path to allow for pruning and planting.

Beyond the primary design aesthetics, many small touches make this landscape appear to be an image from the past. The entryway gate has a heart of steel but a facade of wood to give it a natural, old-fashioned look. Window boxes perched on wrought-iron railings were re-created from historic photographs of the house.

The gardens at this estate may seem to have been transported out of a coffee-table book about British gardens. But they provide proof that a mixed garden of annuals, perennials, roses, shrubs, and trees works equally well in the Midwest, as long as the plants chosen are well suited for the climate.

Seven

THE WATER'S EDGE

When spring arrives and the skies open up with torrents of rain, it may be hard to praise the Midwest's water wealth. But wealth it is. The region's regular rainfall is the envy of those who live in drought-prone areas of the Southwest and West Coast.

Natural water features abound in the Midwest, making a striking impression on young and old alike. Brooks carve sunlit openings in a forest

A well-designed water garden can combine natural rock formations with intriguing plant combinations.

A small pool reflects the colors of nearby catmint and hardy geraniums.

canopy. Larger streams captivate with swirling pools and sparkling rapids. Waterfalls slip over protruding rocks, their banks clad in cardinal flowers and bee balm. Ponds teem with bluegills and bass while spacious lakes provide sport for swimmers and boaters.

With water inevitably comes wildlife. Mallards may nest near any calm water, sometimes even resting on docked boats or jet skis. Less desirable are Canada geese, which flock to Midwestern ponds. Songbirds also are drawn to water, where they drink, splash, and bathe in the shallows.

In fact, aquatic areas are rich with life, from tiny schools of silvery minnows to nightly choruses of spring peepers.

With these kinds of experiences being a natural part of many Midwesterners' upbringings, what could be more appropriate than to add water to the garden?

A quiet pool reflects the blue sky, white clouds, and surrounding greenery while revealing rocks and fish in its transparent depths. It adds new horizons to the garden.

"The basic elements needed to live are sun, plants, and water, the first two being obvious in any garden, while water will only put on a show if captured in a basin or water garden. Putting a water feature into a garden provides a sense of completion," says landscape designer Kathy Stokes-Shafer.

The flow of a stream provides hypnotic motion akin to the flickering flames of a campfire.

The bubbling music of water spilling from fountains or cascading down spillways filters out the sounds of cars and other reminders of urban life.

Bringing the beauty of these natural elements into your yard can be done with the help of landscape designers and landscape architects. They can design waterfalls, reflecting pools, and even streams for your yard, setting them in dramatic rocky banks and filling in around them with flowers and foliage.

This chapter is devoted to the water gardens developed in northeast Ohio by the Pattie Group of Novelty, Ohio, one of the top firms in the region when it comes to water features. In addition, you'll get tips on creating a native bog garden, with examples from Holden Arboretum in Kirtland, Ohio.

The Pattie Group Approach

Dramatic water features have been a specialty of the Pattie Group since the late 1980s, but were brought to the public eye in a big way when the group designed the world's largest indoor waterfall for Floralscape '95, a spring exposition in Cleveland, Ohio. The accolades have continued as the Pattie Group received three 1997 Associated Landscape Contractors of America Awards for design excellence of their water gardens.

Steve Pattie, owner and landscape designer, credits much of the

Kathy Stokes-Shafer, Steve Pattie, and Dana Owens make up the design team for the Pattie Group.

The progress of each major project is shown on a storyboard, which combines the design plan with photographs of installations. This helps keep all staff members—from maintenance crews to designers—up-to-date.

Group's success to teamwork between garden designer Kathy Stokes-Shafer, who incorporates herbaceous plants into designs, and landscape architect Dana Owens, who translates design ideas into blueprints. The Pattie Group team also includes in-house construction and maintenance personnel, all of whom contribute to the finished garden.

Well-trained crews with artistic sensibilities work at every level of the design and installation process—from initial sketches to the placement of the rocks. Designers go out into the field to help with the initial layout, finessing their landscape plan to ensure that it takes on the perspective they imagined.

"The landscape blueprint accounts for about 80 percent of the creation of the initial image, while the installation accounts for another 10 percent, and maintenance of the plants as they mature over the next several years provides the finishing touches and final 10 percent of the image," Pattie says.

The Dramatic Waterfall

To enjoy sheer power, visit towering Brandywine Falls in Boston Heights, Ohio, where a silver torrent of water drops over a steep rock cliff. Or listen to the thundering roar of the rain-swollen Chagrin River where it pours over the Chagrin Falls. A sheet of water, slipping down gentle, layered steps of shale like a sheet of transparent satin, can be just as dynamic, only in a quieter way.

In winter, a waterfall takes on an equally intriguing persona. If the water remains running, ice cascades down over rocks, forming frozen masses that resemble molten lava. Rocky banks clad in evergreen Christmas ferns and partridgeberry provide welcome color and interesting structure in contrast to barren tree trunks and silhouettes of naked limbs.

Created waterfalls can have all the beauty of natural falls with an added advantage—they can be strategically placed to give the most impact in the landscape. Situated near a patio or often-used window, they can be enjoyed from indoors and out. If a window is left open, the sound of cascading water will drift indoors as well.

A waterfall can be custom designed to fit your own idea of beauty. You can choose sound levels, from soft and musical trickles to strong and insistent flows, captivating the ears as well as the eyes.

You can also influence the rhythmic movement of water by curving the spillway, with water glancing off one rock and splashing onto another. On a placid, flat, and otherwise featureless site, this kind of bold action is a scene-stealer.

A waterfall alone, however, is not enough. It needs to be placed in a setting that ties it to the yard and makes it look natural. As a stream strips away soft earth, depositing it in rich, silty layers down-stream, it reveals stones below, which form the basis of the waterfall and its protective banks.

Falling water adds a new dimension to the garden.

Building boulder-strewn banks is just part of the art and craft of waterfall design. The illusion of permanence can be enhanced by clothing the banks and nearby garden areas with naturalistic plantings. These can include low-growing evergreens and clusters of moisture-loving perennials and ferns near the water's edge. Occasional flowering trees and shrubs allow for variations in form and texture, plus seasonal change. Interesting alpines can cluster amid the rocks, as can drought-tolerant herbs and ground covers like thymes and creeping sedums.

The Pattie Group regularly builds planting cylinders into the rocky framework, securing 6-inch-diameter pipes between the rocks. Each pipe is provided with its own irrigation tube, connected to an automatic timer. The pipes are filled with soil appropriate for the desired plant and are kept moist. Soon after planting, the inhabitants begin to bush out and creep over the rocks, softening harsh lines and adding intriguing texture with their silhouetted foliage.

Opposite: Waterfalls give a garden drama, music, and motion.

An Integrated Waterfall

In Russell, Ohio, a waterfall is part of a landscape that is carefully integrated with the house to create a smooth, harmonious look. The quarter-acre front yard blends the waterfall, an entryway, a rock and flower garden, and an outdoor entertaining area. The landscape was planned simultaneously with the house, allowing the Pattie Group to mold the topography, drive, and house placement for the most strategic garden advantage.

When approaching the house, visitors can stop at a parking area where a 4-foot-wide fitted-stone walk arcs up to the front door. It passes beds of golden yarrow, catmint, hardy geraniums, and other perennials. The walkway swells to surround a massive cement planter full of summer tropicals and terminates at the front door, which is bordered on each side with rhododendrons.

A narrower side path of fitted 2-foot-wide stepping stones leads through the perennial garden to the patio and waterfall, which is unseen but not unheard just beyond the crest of a small hill. Stones used as steps are in their natural form, rounded or slightly irregular slabs with great character. They pass a blue, pink, and yellow perennial garden, filled with clusters of pink coralbells and

This water garden blends naturally into a colorful landscape.

Colorful perennial gardens link the front entryway to the side patio and water garden.

dianthus, yellow 'Moonbeam' coreopsis, blue 'May Night' salvia, clustered bellflowers, and 'Butterfly Blue' pincushion flowers, as well as spring-blooming forget-me-nots and azaleas.

Family members and workers usually bypass this entrance. They drive to the garage, circling around the spacious garden, which is walled off from the drive and surrounding woods by a naturalistic planting of hemlocks.

A walk beside the garage leads immediately to the patio, intricately crafted of many-colored pieces of irregularly sized stone. Adjacent to the patio and in line with the French doors of the breakfast room is a striking waterfall. Boulders trail away from the sloping summit of the waterfall to stud the surrounding gardens. As if buried by time or glaciers below a mantle of earth, only a small portion of the stones' upper surfaces is revealed.

This waterfall gracefully splits into two spillways.

Opposite: This waterfall cascades down a natural slope at the edge of a ravine.

Because it is near the house, the waterfall was made intentionally quiet, which enhances the space without overwhelming it. The water, welling up at the top of a 6-foot-tall mounded rise, flows along one of two paths. It can take a short, fast drop in the shelter of semi-evergreen cotoneasters or a long slide down a slight slope, past red, cut-leaf Japanese maples and golden 'Sum and Substance' hostas, to spill off a rough, tiered stone outcropping. Spillway pools are flanked with perennial drifts of cool blue, long-blooming 'May Night' salvias, yellow 'Happy Returns' daylilies, and great sweeps of 'Purple Showers' violas.

Enhancing a Ravine

Beside a Tudor house carved into the woods at the crest of a wooded ravine, a new, slightly raw waterfall cascades through a sparkling, sunlit opening. The house appears to have been designed around the waterfall, although in reality just the opposite is true.

The waterfall cascades beside a wooden deck at the summit and sweeps around the side of the house. Its babbling sound can be heard from the adjacent living room and screened porch.

The water emerges from a rock shelf and falls into a kidney-shaped upper pool filled with water lilies. The water then splashes down a rocky gradient, breaks into two streams where a dwarf weeping hemlock occupies a rocky ledge, and crashes down off a small cliff into a pool below.

Even when the rocks were new, they looked as if they had been in place forever. But some of the greenery—junipers and ivy, in particular—is still young and has not yet cemented the finished image into place. The rockwork is framed with repeated plantings

"Our clients lead hectic lives and need a place to escape when they get home. A water garden provides that. Anyone can walk into the back yard, hear the tranquil sound of the babbling waterfall, and let their workday slip away," says Steve Pattie.

of red cut-leaf Japanese maples, creeping blue junipers, ostrich ferns, and rhododendrons, an appealing mix for all four seasons.

Rock steps that appear to be carved into the hillside lead down beside the waterfall and around to the front of the house. 'Bridal Veil' astilbes, Japanese painted ferns, and small golden hostas squeeze between the rock steps, making an intriguing blend of quiet color and foliage texture. The lower pool is enveloped in daylilies, azaleas, and hostas, which thrive in light shade.

A Waterfall for an Intimate Entertaining Area

In a quiet, flat yard—like those found throughout the Midwest—a waterfall can be a dynamic way to break up the landscape and pro-

A landscape mound and waterfall create the wall of an outdoor living room.

vide interesting topography. This waterfall is the backdrop for a brick terrace, in a side yard just outside the kitchen and breakfast room picture windows. The waterfall is inset into a curving earthen mound, which screens the terrace and water garden from the spreading back yard. The terrace also adjoins the driveway but is secluded from it by a white lattice fence.

The waterfall winds through a framework of mugo pines, weeping hemlocks, and gold-tipped junipers, one such specimen strategically located at each turn. The plantings provide an interesting combination of colors and textures in a rhythm that draws the eye along the waterway. They also partly obscure the view of the water so the entire waterfall is not revealed at once. Seeing the entire run, from top to bottom, requires viewing from several angles.

A sweep of ostrich ferns graces the top of the mound and falls, with a screening blend of 'Roseum Elegans' rhododendrons, crabapples, and conifers providing a backdrop. Around the pool banks, soft clusters of lady's mantle, impatiens, and forget-me-nots contrast with spiky upright 'Perry's Blue' Siberian iris. Tiny tadpoles mill around in the shallow water, promising festive serenades to come.

A Reflecting Pool

One Pattie Group project features a reflecting pool with an air of Oriental intrigue. It is the highlight of a mixed border that passes between a swimming pool carved into an opening in the woods and pool house.

The pond is two-lobed, reminiscent of a figure eight. The upper lobe, which is the sunnier of the two, holds tropical water lilies. The narrow waist between the two pools allows water to trickle slowly from the top pool to the bottom and provides an anchoring point for an arching, wooden Japanese bridge. Nearby, a stone Japanese lantern adds more Eastern flavor.

The garden surrounding the pool includes a blend of plants for sun and shade and for foliage and flowers. Red cut-leaf Japanese maple, ostrich fern, and clusters of low, mounded 'Little Princess' Japanese spirea provide color in spring, summer, and fall.

The quiet waters of this garden pool are well-suited to water lilies.

Reflections on Aquatic Plants

Not every water feature has to be musical and mobile. Some people prefer a quiet reflecting pool that shows the mirror images of flowers and foliage. Quiet waters are better suited for growing water plants—bright water lilies with their floating leaves, water cannas with tall spikes of bright flowers, Japanese and Siberian swamp irises, elephant-ear-shaped leaves of tropical taro, and whorled clusters of spiky umbrella palm leaves.

To house this kind of aquatic extravaganza, a pool needs water of an appropriate depth. Water lilies need quiet water that is 6 to 18 inches deep. Bog plants grow in shallower water and can be settled on shelves molded into the sides of the water garden or placed on inverted pots in deeper water.

Tropical water lilies, both fragrant and floriferous, need more than half a day of direct sun and warm temperatures, preferably over 80 degrees F. Unfortunately, they are not hardy, but this gives you the opportunity to try new varieties every year. You can choose between day and night bloomers with flowers of yellow, pink, white, purple, and blue.

Bog plants, which can envelop the perimeter of the water garden and give it a natural boundary, come in an interesting assortment of shapes, sizes, and colors. There are classics like sagittaria, with its upright leaves and cute white flowers, and cattails that are slender and upright with the characteristic woolly brown seed spikes. There also are choices with vivid leaves—variegated taro with mottled elephant-ear foliage, variegated cannas with gold, red, and orange striping, and houttuynia, a creeper with leaves of red, green, and maroon.

These plants are best submerged within pots, and require special aquatic soils and fertilizers.

An elegant lotus holds its flowers high over its leaves.

Tips for Water Garden Construction and Maintenance

The artistic and design implications of water features would come to little more than fanciful ideas if the mechanics of building,

"After installing the waterfall, we often are called back to a landscape to install fire pits or lighting. People are drawn outside and want to enjoy the waterfall at any hour," says Steve Pattie.

powering, and plumbing a waterfall or pond were neglected. Equipment is needed to fill the water garden, take excess water away, and circulate it.

The Pattie Group begins every water garden on a mechanical level—installing pipes, overflow drains that prevent flooding, and electrical components. Once the plumbing and other underground elements are installed, lawns, trees, and shrubs can be added around the water garden.

For water conservation, include an automatic water refill feature, Steve Pattie suggests. The device works like the tank on a toilet: When the water drops below a certain level, the automatic refill adds new water. This keeps water for any type of water feature continually flowing and prevents damage to the pump.

A pump can be internal, buried in a utility area below the ground with an access door hidden under a rock. Or it can be external, enclosed in a building or cave carved into a berm. While internal pumps can remain in place, except for occasional servicing, external pumps need to be taken into a cool but protected place for winter and stored in a bucket of water to help preserve the seals. Even with the best care, Pattie says, pumps seldom last more than several years before requiring replacement.

It's important to line the bottom of the water garden with a material that won't rupture and allow the water to leak out. Pattie avoids plastic liners, some of which can be easily broken. He prefers to use 45 ml rubber liners, available from roofing supply houses. They are laid over a foundation of fiber-cloth matting, and topped and protected with a 2-inch layer of concrete, painted an inconspicuous brown. Another option is to build the water garden base like a swimming pool, with concrete on a rebar skeleton. This is a better choice where dogs or kids will be running through the water, which can increase the possibility of a lining tear.

Although water gardens need no weeding or watering, they do require maintenance. Regularly check the pH—the acidity or alkalinity of the water—keeping it on the alkaline side. This prevents algae "blooms," green clouds in the water that occur when nutrients are released in acidic water. An algicide may be necessary to keep the water clear.

Each spring, before starting up the water feature for that year, drain it and vacuum out the leaves and algae, using a vacuum designed for wet areas. If you have fish or tadpoles, cover the pump openings with wire mesh so they won't be pulled in.

A Bog Garden of Rarities

Unique bogs found here and there through the Midwest are rich environments for the growth of rare and endangered plants and can make a quite interesting naturalistic garden, as evidenced at the Holden Arboretum in Kirtland, Ohio. This swampy garden, traversed on wooden pallet steps, includes low, creeping shrubs such as leatherleaf and large cranberry, which bears very sour but beautiful

Above: The hardy pitcher plant, shown here in fruit, is a rare insect-eating plant. Insects crawl down the leafy tubes and are held in the bottom by downward-pointing hairs until they are digested.

Left: The beautiful foliage of this large cranberry laps over wooden pallet steps.

and large red berries that can linger on the plant for a year or more. Other options include the lush mottled chain fern and the poster child of the bog, the pitcher plant.

To make a bog in a low-lying area, you can line the garden floor with 12 mm plastic or 45 ml rubber liners. Top the liner with silica sand and peat moss, which will help to create the required acidic conditions.

Eight

ANNUALS FOR A TASTE OF THE TROPICS

ast-blooming, flashy annuals are celebratory, like birthday streamers and balloons or brilliant explosions of fireworks on the Fourth of July. Just shopping for annuals in the spring, browsing through greenhouses brimming with jewel-bright selections, is uplifting. These mere seedlings, held in modest packs or pots, come wrapped in hope and excitement for the beauties they will become as they grow.

In the Midwest, tulips can provide this kind of spectacular performance if treated like annuals. Remove the faded bulbs after they finish blooming and plant fresh bulbs each fall.

Annuals tend to be easy to grow and long-blooming. Coloring the garden instantly and with flamboyance, they can enliven a wide range of landscapes and are suitable for changing whenever the mood strikes.

Planting an annual garden is one thing many amateur gardeners can do well. But where time or desire to do it yourself is lacking, garden designers may be called upon to incorporate annuals into clients' gardens. Designers, unlike some amateurs, know how to integrate annuals into the overall landscape. Their location, color, height, texture, and other characteristics must be carefully assessed to add emphasis to garden highlights, rather than to prove a colorful distraction.

Designers who specialize in flowers will have an expanded palette of annuals from which to choose, using the newest and best plants and concocting sensational color combinations.

In a traditional landscape, annual flowers may be planted in clusters in the foundation planting, set in pots on the front steps, lined into edgings around vegetable and herb gardens, set in rows in cutting gardens, or given beds all their own for luminescent patterned plantings. Influenced by a rising popularity in cottage gardens, some designers blend self-seeding, old-fashioned annuals—larkspurs, cleome, annual poppies—amid flowering shrubs, fragrant roses, perennials, and arbors dripping with wisteria and trumpet creeper.

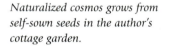

Naturalized cosmos grows from self-sown seeds in the author's cottage garden.

Annuals are not all static summer bloomers as popularly imagined. The group also includes frost-hardy spring and fall bloomers
such as pansies, sweet alyssum, and lobelias. Tropical vines and
foliage plants, such as 'Blackie' sweet-potato vine, with its purple-
black leaves, and coleus, with its multicolored foliage, also are
increasingly popular. In the Midwest, you must also include tulips
and chrysanthemums, often planted for the glory of a single season.
If they survive and perform well for a second year, that is an unex-
pected bonus.

Botanical gardens, brilliant showplaces of annuals, are excellent
sources for designer ideas. Two of the three designers highlighted
in this chapter—Doug Hoerr, consulting landscape architect for the
Chicago Botanic Garden, and Jane Rogers of Cantigny Gardens in
Wheaton, Illinois—show their talents at public gardens. The third,
Michelle D'Arcy, owns a landscape maintenance firm and is a container garden innovator in the Chicago area, where she works for
private clients.

*Crimson Joseph's coat, blue
salvia, orange cosmos, and
green burning bush (which
turns scarlet in autumn) make
a festive display.*

A Parade of Bedding Schemes

Hundreds of varieties of annuals can be massed into free-form sweeps or formal geometric patterns that paint color across the landscape. How to blend these flowers into contrasting or harmonious color schemes and how to mix their height and foliage to best advantage are variables that designers delight in.

Compact low-growers such as vining 'Purple Wave' petunias and 'Imagination' verbena spread across the front of a garden, around taller plants, or over the side of a pot. Bedding annuals like impatiens, 'Gypsy' baby's-breath, ageratums, and fibrous-rooted begonias are gracefully mounded and good to plant in masses. Salvias, flowering tobaccos, and wheat-type celosias have upright flower spikes, dramatic to mingle with lower forms.

An intriguing sample of design options can

Above: 'Janie Primrose' marigolds surround 'Cirrus' dusty-miller at Cantigny Gardens in Wheaton, Illinois.

Right: An assortment of ideas for great annual combinations are displayed side by side.

be experienced at Cantigny Gardens. Cantigny, the estate of former *Chicago Tribune* publisher Robert R. McCormick, was developed into a 500-acre park that is open to the public. Amid the ten acres of formal gardens are dozens of beds of annuals blended in formal and traditional arrays of dazzling colors.

Jane Rogers, annual flower designer for Cantigny, says the gardens showcase the best annuals for the Midwest. Each variety in the formal plantings has been proven to be a top performer in trials at Cantigny or other local gardens before it is considered for the main garden. New annuals are introduced each year, but many of the old reliable varieties return to be planted in innovative new designs.

Annual garden beds loop under trees and arc in quadrants around a circular fountain. They also form a huge spiral through which one can stroll for an hour, looking at all the flowers and color blends.

One of the most interesting sections of the annual garden features eleven rectangular beds about 10 feet wide and 17 feet long. They nestle side by side, backing up to clipped boxwood hedges. These beds show a variety of ways to blend annuals of similar heights but of varying colors and textures. The designs are simple but create distinct and striking impressions.

"To keep these rectangular beds fresh, we vary the planting patterns in each bed," Rogers says. "I plan each design a year ahead. But when I actually lay the plants out in spring and see their real-life colors and forms, I sometimes find myself making changes to show them off better."

Solo beds of 'Floral Lace Picotee' dianthus, with white-fringed red petals circling a white eye, and another of 'Storm' coleus, with scalloped leaves, a heart of green, tips of gold, and red splotches

Top: 'Pinwheel Salmon' and 'Pinwheel White' zinnias mingle in an informal planting.

Above: A single bed is devoted to vivid 'Storm' coleus.

throughout, show how a single, multicolored annual can be as vibrant as a mixed bed. The colorful cultivars also suffer no conflicts with ill-mated companions. A large cluster can accent a doorway, point the way to a far-off garden path, or sweep along the front of a shrub border.

The other Cantigny beds combine two compatible annuals, planted in varying patterns.

❧ Staggered squares of boldly contrasting 'Starship Burgundy' and 'Starship White' flowering tobacco make a strongly rhythmic, formal pattern.

❧ A drought-resistant planting of vincas features a central oval—shaped like an old-fashioned mirror—of 'Heatwave Pink', surrounded by an edging of 'Heatwave White', all neatly uniform and floriferous.

❧ A broad "S" curve of upright 'Liberty Yellow' snapdragons is enveloped by a curvy, thick carpet of 'Flash Pink Center' petunias. The combination has a soft but controlled feel.

More informal beds blend different colors of the same cultivar, matching flower form and shape. The

Above: Yellow snapdragons wind through a bed of pink petunias.

Right: Strong contrasting colors and cubic planting patterns make a bold scheme.

bright daisylike faces of disease-resistant 'Pinwheel Salmon' and 'Pinwheel White' zinnia make natural companions for a casual garden. Mixed spikes of elegant, lean blue salvias and lush red salvias make for a beautiful blend of warm and cool colors. When edged with a low white flower such as nierembergia, they are the makings of a patriotic red, white, and blue garden.

'Apricot Brandy' cockscomb contrasts with 'Dreams Midnight' petunia.

For a taller meadow garden or a high-flying mixture between newly planted perennials, try tall blends of 'White Queen' and 'Violet Queen' cleome, with long-legged stamens as attractive as the colored petals.

As in a perennial garden, you also can interplant annuals of different heights, forms, and textures. These spirited and intricate

Heliotrope, petunias, and nierembergia make an attractive, informal blend.

mixtures invite contemplation of the contrasts and harmonies. One Cantigny combination blends a low edging of white, open-faced 'Mount Blanc' nierembergia with arching blue clusters of 'Marine' heliotrope and petite flowers of 'Fantasy Pink Morn' petunia. This grouping becomes even more intriguing with the influence of nearby apricot portulaca, golden Dahlberg daisies, yellow snapdragons, and blue ageratums.

135

Mixed violas make a cheerful spring basket.

Potted Annuals

Whether you have a garden in your yard or not, you can showcase a blend of annuals in a large container garden—an urn, pot, or tub kept on a patio, on steps, or by a door. Some designers specialize in the detail work of making intriguing containers and turn an ordinary pot into a work of living art.

Once such person is Michelle D'Arcy, a horticulturist with her own garden specialty company, Horticultural Associates Inc., in Gurnee, Illinois. In addition to planting and tending flower gardens, she creates interesting combinations of annuals and perennials in her clients' favorite containers. Designed to bring colors of the garden to the house, and vice versa, these containers make useful transitions between indoors and out, between garden areas and patios.

When selecting plants, D'Arcy considers the style of the container, the surroundings, and the building materials used. She plans whether the container will act as a focal point or blend in with the surroundings.

"I try to follow the same basic design criteria in my pots as in an overall landscape design," D'Arcy says.

Each pot becomes a miniature garden, crafted with careful blends of foliage textures and plant forms to give mixed pots interesting greenery all summer. Flowers in a tailored range of colors and heights also can look good together in the close confines of a pot.

"Not limiting myself to certain types of plants adds to the creativeness of the pots. I love to mix all types—tropicals, herbs, grasses, perennials, ground covers, and shrubs," D'Arcy says.

A large urn on a stone terrace mixes the finely cut foliage and spilling yellow flowers of 'Moonbeam' coreopsis with more upright, feathery-leaved pink and white cosmos. The wide leaves of sweet basil and occasional blades of grass form a striking contrast.

A poolside green stoneware pot holds purple-leaved coralbells encircling feathery white cosmos and blue bachelor's-buttons.

A dynamic doorway planting in a weathered terra-cotta pot makes a terrific way to say, "Welcome." Large plumes of 'Kimberly Queen' Boston fern, nestled in the shade next to the house, stand above a vivid red-leaved caladium. The color spectrum shifts toward the front of the pot, where white-leaved caladium and cascading golden-leaved vines of 'Limelight' helichrysum predominate.

For an upright urn molded in a classic Greek form, D'Arcy complements the rise of the container with airy purple fountain grass feathered with pink flower spikes. 'Blackie', a purple-black sweet-potato vine, underplants the fountain grass, draping around the sides of the pot.

To extend the lifetime of a container planting, keep the pot consistently moist, D'Arcy says. She also recommends fertilizing with Peter's Blossom Booster every two weeks and grooming the plants regularly—removing faded flowers and foliage and pinching back lanky stems. If one plant refuses to cooperate and grow well, replace it with another.

An Ingenious Annual Garden

The Chicago Botanic Garden's Circle Garden exemplifies what annuals do best: provide quick color. Created during the summer of 1997, the magnificent garden was filled with abundant color by late summer, thanks to tropical lantanas, silver-leaved Swedish ivy,

The Chicago Botanic Garden's Circle Garden uses tulips to provide riotous spring color.

purple-leaved castor beans, blue-spiked salvias, and willowy purple Brazilian verbenas. It seemed almost as if the garden had magically appeared in full-grown glory overnight.

The planting scheme changes through the seasons, glowing with tulips, stock, pansies, and other cool-season annuals in spring and shifting to tropical annuals for summer and early fall. Cool-season annuals return in late fall.

The garden, a formal affair, centers on a sparkling fountain with thirty-two upright water plumes that dance in a variety of patterns and heights. A central walkway is sliced in two by a bold cubical pattern of square, clipped boxwood. Alternating plantings of two cultivars are used—'Glencoe' boxwood with 'Wintergreen' boxwood. In dramatic contrast, the walkway is skirted with soft blends of annuals, such as creeping golden sweet potato vines and clumps of spider plants or sweeps of purple and yellow violas with tall spikes of fragrant white-flowered stock and dangling purple bells of fritillary.

The fountain is embellished with its own bed of uniquely interplanted annuals, eye-catching combinations with potential for any home garden. In the garden's first spring, it beckoned with a cheery blend of yellow, purple, and orange-red tulips; golden pansies; and contrasting blue grape hyacinths. Summer followed with 'Sulfur' sweet potato, spiky dracaena, and standard tree lantanas. In fall, cold-hardy kale added interest to the mix.

The main portion of the garden backs up to hedges of Hicks yew and early blooming Cornelian cherry dogwoods, effectively veiling secret gardens that arise down smaller side paths. These intimate garden rooms are further walled in with a thick border of trees and shrubs—spring-blooming 'Merrill' magnolia, 'Froebelii' spirea, 'Mohican' viburnum, 'Remontii' Norway spruce, mugo pine, and informal clusters of 'Wintergreen' boxwood.

Above: In April, tulips and Persian fritillary mix with fragrant stocks.

Below: In summer, the garden glows with 'Indian Summer' coneflowers, 'Sunny Red' cosmos, classic zinnias, and Brazilian verbenas.

A formal garden layout harbors surprising blends of annuals.

The annuals grown here—within a stiff, boxy bed—could not be more exuberant, mingling with each other and straining to burst out of the confines of the garden. Castor beans with leaves of burgundy complement the purple balls of 'Confetti' lantana and the rose, white, and pink of 'Daylight Sensation' flowering tobacco. The corners of the bed are trimmed in spider plants with their arching leaves of green and cream. Typically grown as houseplants,

Ruby-tinted castor bean leaves provide bold splashes of color beside more fine-textured Brazilian verbena, fountain grass, and cosmos.

spider plants may seem remarkable in an outdoor setting, but they grow easily outdoors and add character.

The garden also has been decked out in purple Brazilian verbena, orange tiger lilies, silver 'Powis Castle' artemisia, and trailing lantana.

"The garden had a strong existing shape and powerful design, so I didn't need to divide the beds into individual planting areas or parterres [formal, patterned European-style plantings]. I wanted to keep the spaces as large as possible and blend within them a playful interpretation of the meadows, prairies, and ponds in nearby areas of the botanical garden," says Doug Hoerr, consulting landscape architect.

Some of Hoerr's playful combinations include the following:

❧ Drifts of silver-leaved Swedish ivy with brilliant red Joseph's coat, an upright form with dark red leaves at the base and fuchsia-red leaves bubbling up at the top.

❧ 'Sulfur' sweet potato, purple Brazilian verbena, and large purple-flowered onion.

❧ Orange-red dahlias, red-leaved Joseph's coat, graceful *Zinnia angustifolia* 'Gold Star', and wildly irregular, upright stems of kochia.

'Carmencita' castor bean, Brazilian verbena, and 'Peaches and Cream' verbena fill a secret side garden.

OTHER ANNUAL IDEAS

✼

Beyond the Circle Garden, the Chicago Botanic Garden's main island abounds with display gardens that introduce new and better plant varieties and showcase trend-setting plant combinations and design ideas.

In 1998, these annuals were in bright bloom:

White 'Carnegie' hyacinths bloom with 'Passionale Purple' tulips.

❧ Mixes of simultaneously blooming bulbs highlighted garden walks and entrances. The array included pink, cream, yellow, orange, and red tulips underplanted by orange, red, and yellow ranunculus; white 'Carnegie' hyacinths; and 'Passionale Purple' tulips.

❧ Container gardens, with intense blends of foliage and dynamic color schemes, provided drama

This miniature white garden contained in a pot includes stocks, primroses, and ranunculus.

in pavilions, on steps and walks, and at building entrances. A brilliant pot of white flowers—glowing in the spring sun—combined fragrant white stock, rounded ranunculus flowers, silver-leaved dusty miller, flat-faced white pansies, white-flowered baby blue-eyes, and white primrose.

❧ A Fruit and Vegetable Island proved that annuals can look and taste good. A bright and cheerful annual bed of leafy greens and edible flowers was edged in large sweeps of frilly chartreuse leaf lettuce. The garden was interplanted with bolder-textured, round and red-tipped lettuce heads. These studies in green were highlighted by clumps of upright, golden-stemmed Swiss chard and ruby-red orach with ground-hugging clusters of deep purple pansies.

Mixed cos and 'Grand Rapids' lettuce, pansies, and red orach make a handsome, incredible-edible garden.

❧ Golden-leaved coleus with purple Brazilian vervain and 'Victoria Blue' salvia.

❧ For a simultaneous flowering in spring: 'Daystemon' tarda tulip; 'Princess Irene', 'Red Shine', 'Lightening Sun', 'Red Wing' tulips; and blue spikes of grape hyacinth.

Brightening the Urban Landscape

Doug Hoerr, principal of Douglas Hoerr Landscape Architecture, Inc., in Evanston, Illinois, is a landscape architect with a green thumb as well as a contractor's eye. In the late 1980s Hoerr left his drafting board to take a gardening sabbatical in England. He worked with trendsetting perennial nurseryman Alan Bloom, plantsman Beth Chatto, and designer John Brookes.

"I returned with a new perspective, an understanding and

Doug Hoerr uses interesting blends of foliage in the award-winning planters outside Chicago's Michigan Avenue Crate & Barrel store.

appreciation of the role horticulture can play within landscape architecture," Hoerr says.

As the Chicago Botanic Garden's first consulting landscape architect, Hoerr was in charge of devising annual combinations for the Circle Garden. He and his talented staff also designed the median planters for Chicago's Michigan Avenue, as well as the seasonal display gardens for Crate & Barrel stores in Chicago, Dallas, Washington, D.C., and New York City.

"These urban gardens are challenging projects for us," Hoerr says. "We are handed small leftover areas within the architectural framework of the city. Using only plants, the gardens must be powerful enough to hold their own against the backdrop of world-famous architecture."

In addition to designing, he lectures and teaches at the Chicago Botanic Garden, the Morton Arboretum, and the Chicago Architecture Foundation.

Nine

PERENNIAL PARADISE

꿍

erennials were among the first ornamentals to be planted by European settlers. In addition to the array of European perennials bundled across the country in covered wagons, native perennials—asters, coneflowers, and goldenrods—were added to the earliest American cottage gardens.

Perennial seeds, cuttings, divisions, and bulblets were passed between friends and neighbors.

Opposite: Dramatic contrasts in foliage form highlight this rock garden designed by June Hutson.

Peonies have been Midwestern favorites for decades.

gardening. They died back to the ground, where they were safe from the Midwestern winter cold and wind chill, but then returned to the garden year after year.

It wasn't long before a variety of Midwestern perennial nurseries arose and the selection of perennials available to early gardeners skyrocketed. In 1852, Klehm Nursery was founded in the Chicago area by bricklayer John Klehm. Originally a Christmas tree farm and vegetable market garden, it evolved to a source of fancy hybrid peonies, hostas, daylilies, and other perennials.

In the early 1920s Wayside Gardens was formed by plant collectors J.J. Grullemans and Elmer Schultz of Mentor, Ohio, to offer

Native perennials such as golden coneflowers and purple coneflowers were natural additions to early flower gardens.

Hostas, shown emerging amid flowering daffodils, will fill in and hide the fading foliage of spring-flowering bulbs.

the best American and European perennials. Although the business moved to Hodges, South Carolina, after being sold in 1975, the Schultz family remains in the nursery business, growing an extensive line of perennials at Springbrook Gardens.

In 1893, Chicago-based Vaughans Seed Store put out a mail-order catalogue with all kinds of seeds and nursery plants. The store promoted the idea of an old-fashioned garden, featuring hollyhocks, shady walks, and many of the dozens of perennials they had for sale.

"The Grand field of Horticulture (that 'Art which doth mend nature') contains too many high class flowers and plants to justify us in offering inferior or worthless articles . . . ," the Vaughans catalogue boasted.

After this grand beginning, perennial gardening popularity lost ground to annuals for a time. But a perennial resurgence began in the late 1970s, ushered in on the wings of East Coast designers James Van Sweden and Wolfgang Oehme, who use meadowlike drifts of such perennial all-stars as 'Goldsturm' golden coneflower, violet sage, 'Autumn Joy' sedum, and ornamental grasses. Another person setting the perennial wave in motion has been St. Louis designer Ken Miller, whom you will meet in this chapter.

Right: Orange butterfly weed contrasts with blue balloon flower.

Below: Old-fashioned bleeding-heart flowers in spring and usually lies dormant in summer.

Today, landscape designers are slipping perennials into evergreen foundation plantings, making perennial borders, cottage gardens, and island beds. The perennials provide simple or complex color schemes, which can change through the seasons as new perennials come into bloom. For continuous color through the season, a well-planned design is crucial.

Perennial-garden designers can be found throughout the Midwest. Some enhance the landscape with a few large clusters of high-performance perennials. Others focus on creating complex perennial gardens of elaborate artistry. In this chapter, you'll see the work of designer June Hutson as well as Ken Miller. For these professionals, and other designers, perennials are an important part of multifaceted landscape plans.

A Perennial Cottage Garden

Creating a perennial garden with layer upon layer of flowers staged for maximum effect requires experience, careful juggling, and a fine sense of timing. All of these are present in Ken Miller's dramatic perennial gardens.

In Kirkwood, Missouri, Miller transformed the entryway to a brick-fronted ranch house into an intricate cottage garden.

Entered through a trim, white crossrail fence, a rust, tan, and cream stone walk curves in an "S" before arcing to the front door. It passes a hemlock and several yews, all that remain of the once-traditional foundation planting.

The glory of the garden in early summer is 'Moonshine' yarrow, which is repeated rhythmically beside the curves in the walk. Its flat flower buds have a silvery sheen but quickly change to sun-warmed

In early summer 'Moonshine' yarrow dominates Nancy Ellis' cottage garden.

Lamb's-ears provides contrast with its furry silver foliage.

gold as they open. Lower-growing 'Sunray' coreopsis and airy 'Moonbeam' coreopsis echo the sunny hues.

Contrasts in color and form invite visitors to look closely as they walk to the door or drive by. Purple Siberian iris, with spiky upright leaves, stand near the fence, which is covered with pink 'William Baffin' climbing rose, one of the hardiest and best climbing roses for the Midwest, and pink 'Nelly Moser' clematis. Pink-purple flowers of bloody cranesbill, purple foliage of 'Palace Purple' coralbells, and pink flowers of silver-leaved lamb's ears provide color reverberations across the garden.

Near the front door, the garden lights up with white flowers. An oakleaf hydrangea, with pyramidal clusters of pristine white flowers and oak-lobed leaves, is underplanted with a ribbon of green hosta. Across the path, white penstemons arise from amid a clump of 'Palace Purple' coralbells and large, blue-leafed hosta.

The owner's favorite perennial—lady's-mantle—sprays small, frilly chartreuse clusters of flowers just below her front step. An old-fashioned flower with pleated, lightly furred leaves, lady's-mantle boasts foliage that is almost as pretty as its flowers.

For spring, Miller has planned companionable blends of peonies with clematis, willow bluestar, and white, pink, and lavender hardy geraniums. Later in summer, the garden undergoes a dramatic color change with lavender spires of Russian sage and pink-flowered obedient plant. By fall, the color scheme is monopolized by pink and white Japanese anemones, asters, and roses.

"A row of boring meatball evergreens lined up in front of this house would not be appropriate. Ranch houses are more reminiscent of prairies. Low stretches of flowering perennials are just the right look here," Miller says.

In the rear of the two-acre property is an open woods dominated by red and white oaks and undercut with meandering mulched paths. The lawn and woods are edged with perennials. Variegated, gold, and blue hostas spread in huge sweeps, amid

A stone patio nestles the edge of an oak woodland.

feathery pink plumes of 'Irrlicht' astilbe, Siberian irises, azaleas, and English ivy. In an isolated corner of the yard, a stone patio becomes a miniature garden room partly walled in with hemlocks and furnished with a green swing seat, a green wicker chair, and pots of annuals.

In all, this perennial-driven landscape provides a wonderful place for the owner to enjoy her hobby of gardening, to entertain, or to relax.

Setting a Dramatic Stage for Perennials

A large deck overlooks Delia Garcia's backyard perennial garden.

Perennials have traditionally been enjoyed in a border-like setting, surrounded by other perennials, annual flowers, or a few woody plants. But they also can star in more complex geoscapes, says designer Ken Miller. Blended into slopes along with dramatic boul-

ders and evergreens, perennials soften the hardscape and show off attributes that might be lost in the crowd in a thickly planted border.

At a suburban home in Town and Country, Missouri, Miller has converted a steep slope into a dramatic sandstone rock garden. It is entered on stairs leading down from a pergola-covered deck and overlook. A perennial-clad path loops down the slope on steps made of stone slabs and terminates at a summerhouse.

Dwarf conifers edge the walk, along with low, spreading 'Repandens' English yews, red filigree-leaf Japanese maples, and other extraordinary trees and shrubs, which frame the perennials emerging amid them. Maiden grass, held upright with a nearly invisible corset of crossed bamboo poles, forms a partial screen, adding more intrigue.

Salvia, 'Palace Purple' coralbells, and 'Moonbeam' coreopsis spread beside a stone walk.

This summerhouse is located at the bottom of a hillside.

In early summer, rhythmic bursts of color spread along the walk, with 'Seven Hills Giant' catmint leading the way and clusters of golden 'Moonshine' yarrow and yellow 'Moonbeam' coreopsis always close at hand. Between the rocks bloom brilliant pink-flowered poppy mallow, purple-leaved 'Palace Purple' coralbells, 'East Friesland' salvia, bloody cranesbill, 'Butterfly Blue' scabiosa, and creeping thymes with woolly white foliage or an endless cover of white flowers. Occasional clumps of long-blooming 'The Fairy' polyantha roses and airy lavender spires of Russian sage make perfect companions.

Above: A hose holder helps keep the garden neat.

Below: These perennials stand out against the stone slabs.

By a tall stone bank, a clump of 6-foot-high white-flowered meadowsweet arises, a sweep of hardy geraniums at its feet. A nearby white-flowered hydrangea echoes the pure whiteness against the rusty brown of the sandstone.

The walk ends at a summerhouse, a large white structure with latticework for walls and screening to keep out insects. The summerhouse is surrounded by a mixed garden of azaleas, hydrangeas, and peonies with a backdrop of blue spruce, the original yard occupants that the garden was designed around.

The Roots of Success

Ken Miller began life with a checkered school career, hampered by learning disabilities. But when he worked at a small neighborhood garden shop, he

PERENNIAL ROCK GARDEN ON A MODEST SCALE

Rock gardens need not be extensive to be attractive foils for perennials. Perennials make a big impact in a small backyard rock garden that Ken Miller designed on a slight slope inset with boulders. Evergreen color comes from creeping 'Blue Shore' juniper and tufted, metallic blue 'Blue Chip' juniper growing beside parallel layers of flat stone. For contrast, there are feathery, low-mounded 'Gold Thread' false cypress and neat, tuftlike bird's-nest spruce.

Amid the low shrubs are perennials growing near the steps and feathering up to greater heights farther out. Betony, an old-fashioned favorite, spreads naturally through the garden to display its tall spikes of red flowers here and there. For spring, there are coralbells, peonies, 'Johnson's Blue' geranium, columbines, and daffodils. For summer, color continues with yarrow and salvia, purple coneflowers, and globe thistle. Purple poppy mallow spreads across much of the garden, blooming with large pink flowers that reach only about 12 inches high.

Blending perennials and compact conifers is a successful formula for smaller rock gardens.

Ken Miller confers with client Nancy Ellis in her cottage garden.

started to gain an understanding of his own unique abilities. Originally helping to stack boxes and do other manual work, by age eleven he was managing the store. In the process, he taught himself how to learn, becoming proficient at business, horticulture, and school.

In 1983, Miller was hired by one of the largest subsidized housing agencies in St. Louis, and subsequently taught horticultural job skills to hundreds of unskilled workers. He strove to make the housing projects look as good as country estates, and succeeded in most cases. He taught local laborers how to prune, mow, and apply lawn chemicals, but his teaching went beyond horticulture. He also taught the value of good work habits such as regular job attendance, productivity, and quality of workmanship.

Miller was called on to create designs for problem areas, and discovered many exceptional solutions—ideas that translate well even now in residential and commercial properties.

"I saw every possible mistake that could be made in horticulture," Miller says. "It was an intensive education."

He also organized a series of nationwide perennial symposiums, among the first of what is now a popular forum. He initiated a plan to have greenhouses custom-grow unusual annuals to showcase at his projects.

SOLUTIONS TO COMMON PEST PROBLEMS

Ken Miller's Bug Store offers a customized program of beneficial insect releases—beginning in spring when you plant your bedding annuals and continuing through summer and into fall if necessary. The bug shipments arrive automatically all through the growing season, just in time to head off any new problems.

Here are some of Miller's solutions to common pest problems:

Pest	Predator	Other Controls
Aphids	Ladybugs, lacewings	SunSpray, Neem
Caterpillars	Trichogramma wasps	B.t., diatomaceous earth, pyrethrin, Neem, insecticidal soap, barriers, sulphur dust
Iris borer	Beneficial nematodes	
Japanese beetles		Garlic barrier, Neem, traps
Leaf miners	Parasites, beneficial nematodes	Neem
Mealybugs	Lacewings, mealybug destroyer	SunSpray, insecticidal soap, Neem, traps
Slugs/snails		Traps, diatomaceous earth

Miller also was the first in his area to use beneficial insects to control garden pests, a revolt against all the thousands of pounds of chemicals he had seen used in his supervisory career. In addition to his design business, Miller operates the Bug Store, a St. Louis retail and mail-order operation where he sells beneficial insects and organic garden products.

Since 1990, Miller has focused on residential landscape design, enjoying the freedom to be creative. Miller crafts a new landscape in his mind's eye before bringing it to life on paper and then in three dimensions.

"I first survey clients to get a feel for their needs and preferences. Then I ask them to pull out pictures of what kind of plants and landscapes they like so I can understand their tastes," he says.

He often draws preliminary plans right on site, bringing a stool to the property and moving it to strategic locations to capture the feel and potential of the place. Once he knows the look he wants, he steps back to solve functional problems like drainage, irrigation, and screening undesirable views.

A Perennial Collector's Garden

With so many perennials to grow and new ones being introduced every day, many gardeners are tempted to collect one of each. But too much diversity in a perennial garden without an overall plan can end up looking simply chaotic.

There are ways to satisfy the need to try a variety of perennials and still have a coherent design, however. They are on display at the Missouri Botanical Garden William Kemper Center for Home Gardening in St. Louis. The eight-acre Kemper Center includes a secret garden, city garden, backyard garden, bird garden, fragrance garden, native prairie, butterfly garden, and native rock garden, all created in areas about the size of a typical back yard.

Pink-flowered evening primroses and other perennials grow in the dwarf conifer garden June Hutson designed for the Missouri Botanical Garden.

While the overall layout of the Kemper Center is by Environmental Planning and Design in Pittsburgh, the planting plans within the garden are by June Hutson, field staff supervisor. Hutson uses hundreds of the best perennials for the lower Midwest, including willow-leaf sunflower, blue mist shrub, 'September Charm' Japanese anemone, sky-blue *Salvia azurea*, yellow lupine-like *Thermopsis villosa*, hardy begonia, deciduous ginger, and Chinese forget-me-not.

"This design job was a little like filling in the outlines in a coloring book," Hutson says.

Lamb's-ears emerges amid 'Johnson's Blue' hardy geranium.

To give these gardens balance and rhythm, certain outstanding perennials, flower colors, and foliage plants are repeated throughout each garden. Interesting walls, walks, patios, and other hardscape and a strong framework of woody background plants also help define the space and pull all the perennials together.

The secret garden exemplifies diversity with unity. Surrounded by a hedge of junipers and hemlocks, the garden has a feeling of seclusion. A thick border of perennials encircles a lawn, where a distinctive bronze sculpture depicts a dog meeting a porcupine. The circular border may be the strongest component of the entire garden, as it is edged in a double row of bricks that bolster the effect of its form.

The color scheme is pink, blue, purple, pale yellow, and white, created with many different perennials all carefully chosen for adherence to color. The garden also is carefully stratified, in most places using clusters of five, seven, or nine low perennials in the foreground and taller plants in the back.

The edging of the garden includes pasqueflower with purple spring blooms emerging from hairy buds, pale pink-flowered *striatum* bloody cranesbill, plumbago with blue flowers in late summer, and 'Big Ears' lamb's-ears. One exception is made for one of Hutson's favorite perennials, pale yellow 'Anthea' yarrow, a

'Anthea' yarrow is one of June Hutson's favorite perennials.

taller plant slipped into the foreground to prevent the height groupings from being overly rigid.

In the rear are bigger, bushy bloomers such as 'Sunny Border
Blue' veronica, 'Alaska' shasta daisy, and 'Caesar's Brother' Siberian
iris.

A bench rests in a shady corner, the perfect place to show off
interesting shade plants such as the hardy orchid *Bletilla striata*. It
has flat, broad, grass-like leaves and pinkish-purple, orchid-shaped
flowers in late spring and summer. Hardy geraniums, which tolerate both sun and shade, blue-leaved hostas, and pink-flowered
'Sprite' astilbe mingle nearby.

Teaching Garden Design by Example

June Hutson, a hands-on horticulturist, designer, and veteran staff
member of the Missouri Botanical Garden, has enjoyed gardening
since childhood. As a young mother staying home with her chil-

Above: June Hutson shows off the Kemper Center prairie garden.

Opposite: Echinacea pallida grows in the Kemper Center prairie garden.

dren, she earned an associate degree in horticulture for fun. The junior college where she had enrolled urged her to volunteer at the Missouri Botanical Garden, and she soon landed a job working with exotic plants in the Garden's Mediterranean House.

When the Mediterranean House was torn down and replaced with the Temperate House, Hutson was asked to select the plants and design the garden for it. She also designed and planted a rock and dwarf conifer garden outside the Temperate House.

Development of the Kemper Center in 1991 created new opportunities for Hutson, who jumped at the chance to design and plant a new set of gardens.

"I needed to grow myself and felt this gave me the best opportunity," she says.

It has taken several years and some reshuffling of plants to shape the gardens the way she likes them. This is one advantage of perennials, she says: Most can be moved on a whim.

"No garden is ever finished," Hutson says. "As trees and shrubs, the bones of the garden, are coming into their own, they will gain size and develop a sense of the garden. Perennials and annuals will continually evolve too and so will your changing preferences."

Some of her favorite perennial combinations include the foliage of 'Northern Halo' hosta with Japanese painted fern or the pale pink flowers of *Penstemon digitalis* with *Echinacea pallida*, both duos having similar colors but different textures. Strong contrasts come from chartreuse-leaved hostas with 'Chatterbox' or 'Mt. St. Helens'

DETERRING DEER

❧

Kathy Stokes-Shafer of the Pattie Group and Brian Parsons of Holden Arboretum recommended the following ways to keep deer from browsing on your perennials.

❧ To preserve trilliums, hostas, and other perennial favorites from hungry deer, Parsons fences the garden with 8-foot-high plastic-mesh deer fencing. To control those that find their way in anyhow, he sprays feeding deterrents such as Hinder and Bobex weekly until summer arrives and natural food supplies become more plentiful.

❧ Stokes-Shafer plants perennials that deer are less likely to eat, including the following: fernleaf yarrow, common yarrow, pink yarrow, monkshood, maidenhair fern, anise hyssop, bugleweed, hollyhock, giant onion, golden alyssum, willow amsonia, Solomon's-seal, Christmas fern, violet sage, lavender cotton, green santolina, soapwort, lamb's-ears, germander, creeping thyme, and woolly veronica.

'Mary Potter' crabapples form a garden hedge.

coralbells. More casual combinations include mixed grasses like 'Overdam' feather reed grass, reed canary grass, zebra grass, and little bluestem.

Hutson offers design consultation in her spare time, visiting clients' yards, pointing out prominent features of the site and how they might be used in a design.

She usually begins by considering the lay of the land. Some land may need altering, such as raising low areas or cutting down moderately steep slopes.

If planting near a building, define its character before trying to select appropriate plants, Hutson says. You can use the bones of the garden—horizontal hedges or low, wide-branching crabapples like 'Mary Potter'—to contrast with the upright lines of the building.

Hutson also works with landscape contractors, organizing plantings for their projects. She uses a rough sketch to order the right number of plants but waits for them to arrive to decide on their final placing.

"Tweaking the plants into place is fun and creative," Hutson says. "You have so many crayons in the box and get to choose which ones will be best to create the picture you want."

Ten

GARDEN ROOMS

The outdoors need not always take the form of wide-open spaces—of prairies rolling beneath endless skies. Sometimes even nature carves her landscapes into smaller scenes, cozy openings in a thicket of gray dogwood and staghorn sumac, hedgerows separating farm fields, a brook babbling through water-carved stone ledges.

The walled patio of a townhouse becomes a garden room embellished with espalier, edging beds, and bright containers.

It is only natural that we who spend most of our lives enclosed in manmade walls may choose to take one expansive area and divide it into a series of room-like gardens. Enclosed by fencing, trellises, hedges, berms, or informal clusters of bushes, each separate space can have its own identity, season, function, and aesthetics.

One garden room might be an entertainment area with a brick patio, a barbecue pit, pots of culinary herbs, and benches for the family and guests. Another might be a play area with a swing set for the kids, or a golf green, tennis court, pool, or badminton net. In another part of the yard, the compost pile and garbage cans could be separated into a screened outdoor utility room. There also could be an area for quiet reading or contemplation, with a comfortable seat and walls of rustling leaves to soothe the mind.

Garden rooms can be divided into different color themes, offering something to appeal to everyone in the family. There could be a white and silver garden for night-time viewing, a morning garden of blue and pink flowers, and a vivacious afternoon garden of scarlet and chartreuse. All color conflicts are avoided by their separation into different spaces.

Plant collectors can create garden rooms of individual types of plants—roses, perennials, and dwarf conifers. Each would have its own special charms and varying seasons of interest.

Beyond these functional advantages, garden rooms have a curious emotional appeal. By not revealing the entire yard at a single time, they generate curiosity, surprise, and excitement, like a present in its glittering wrapping. They lure the viewer out into the yard, offering the intrigue of what might lie behind the next row of shrubs or the next wrought-iron gate. This makes the landscape an interactive adventure, instead of just an object to be viewed from afar.

When it comes to creating garden rooms, one of the masters is Chuck Freeman, of Charles W. Freeman, Inc., in the St. Louis area. This chapter is devoted to his intriguing landscapes.

Combining Interior and Exterior Design

A native of Arkansas, Chuck Freeman grew up around his father's wildflower gardens and his mother's cutting and perennial gardens.

When he came to St. Louis in 1964, he put his heritage to work, landscaping his own three-acre yard. With spreading lawns, elegant mixed gardens, herbaceous borders, and woodland gardens of hostas, ferns, trilliums, and thousands of spring-blooming bulbs, it soon became as beautiful as any Southern estate.

Freeman, an advertising executive, enjoyed working in the garden, and his neighbors appreciated the results. In 1980, a friend who drove past Freeman's yard every day coaxed him to use his obvious design talent as a profession.

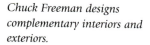

Chuck Freeman designs complementary interiors and exteriors.

Today, Freeman's work speaks volumes beyond what his quiet, polite Southern demeanor would allow. His designs grace estate homes and other properties. He emphasizes informal curving beds and naturalistic plantings but often includes more formal garden areas, edged in boxwood or tall European hornbeam hedges.

"I work very hard to express my clients' tastes instead of pushing my taste on them," Freeman says. "I want them to feel the finished pieces are their own."

Freeman often uses similar color schemes indoors and out, color-coordinating flower gardens to nearby rooms so the view will always be compatible. Sometimes his color choices are remarkable. Freeman called for vivid orange lilies outside a pastel pink and blue living room. When used in flower arrangements in that room, the lilies brought it to life. Blending quiet interiors with bright exteriors is one way to shift the eye to the gardens outdoors, he says.

Freeman calls upon a wide palette of plants with wonderful foliage, flowers, fragrance, or form to create outdoor scenes that can capture the imagination.

He uses many varieties of Japanese maple, including red- and lime-green-leaved forms. Freeman is particularly fond of 'Bloodgood', which holds its color all season, but avoids red-

Bee balm blooms simultaneously with bottlebrush buckeye.

stemmed types, which may suffer bark damage from late spring freezes.

For evergreen interest, Freeman recommends 'China Girl' and 'China Boy' holly, which are both hardy and compact. In addition, many of his garden rooms are edged with low hedges of boxwood, including 'Green Gem', which is extra hardy and stays an attractive green all winter.

Freeman uses climbing hydrangea to scale brick walls or tree trunks. Its handsome oval leaves and large clusters of white flowers always get applause.

Among deciduous shrubs with handsome form, foliage, and flowers, Freeman recommends oakleaf hydrangea, 'Mariesii' doublefile viburnum, and bottlebrush buckeye, with its palmately compound leaves and plumes of white flowers.

With deciduous trees, fragrance is a plus. Some good choices include littleleaf lindens, with their handsome habit and aromatic June flowers; Japanese tree lilacs, with their plumes of white summer flowers; and the southern magnolia, which reminds Freeman of his childhood. It now is available in hardier varieties, such as 'Heaven Scent', appropriate for the lower Midwest.

Appealing to the Senses

Wandering through one of the first gardens Chuck Freeman designed, you cannot help but be impressed by the beauty of the intricate design. But if you close your eyes, you will achieve an entirely different perspective. The tinkle of wind chimes, the trickle of water from a nearby fountain, the sound and feel of the wind rustling through a European hornbeam hedge and ornamental grasses, the scent of fragrant jasmine in a pot beside the pool entice the senses.

This is how Freeman's client, who is blind, experiences the garden. Gentle changes in sound and scent, cool breeze and shadow allow him to orient himself while walking through the garden rooms.

Variegated fallopia grows beside a wrought-iron gate in the brick terrace garden room.

An Italian garden is situated off the perennial garden.

On the side of the house, a brick walk leads past a bed of ivy graced with a unicorn statue cast in stone and wintercreeper euonymus clinging to the trunk of a large pin oak tree. To the right of the walk, an alcove adorned with a wrought-iron mural houses a small garden pool, with water that splashes from a charming terra-cotta frog. Ferns, hostas, and pink impatiens frame the scene and envelop it in natural simplicity.

To the left is a perennial garden, enclosed within a European hornbeam hedge. The perennial border, a casual blend of low-maintenance perennials such as irises, yellow-flowered whorled loosestrife, and bee balm, skirts the hedge. More formal elements—stone urns of Boston ferns by the entrance, and a central fountain edged in hosta beneath a spreading crabapple tree—provide a sense of fanfare.

Two mound-shaped boxwoods stand sentry where an opening in the hedge reveals an Italian garden beyond. It is entered through an elegant, antique French wrought-iron gate accented by large terra-cotta urns of ivy geraniums. The Italian garden, designed according to European tradition, is edged in a mixed border of spruces, Japanese maples, and fine specimen plants underplanted with hostas. The eye is drawn to the far end of the expansive garden, where shafts of sunlight shine over the trees, illuminating a statue of Bacchus surrounded by pink shrub roses.

Behind the house is the entrance to the brick-paved terrace garden. Like the other gardens, this garden combines a layout that is decidedly formal with plantings that are more casual. It is enclosed by brick walls and features two matched rectangular pools with spraying fountains on each side of a central axis. The walls change from a solid panel to brick columns beside a broad stairway leading up to the pool and pool house. A bench made of filigree that is patterned like fern fronds nestles in one corner, beneath the graceful arching limbs of a whitebud tree and beside a hedge of pink azaleas. Garden beds line the walls, most of them edged with neat, low boxwoods or deciduous azaleas.

Although the garden originates at the house, its heart is around the swimming pool and pool house, where the family spends most of their time in summer. A lap pool is set in a stone terrace, abundantly adorned with large, potted tropicals such as hibiscus, fragrant oleanders, and standard jasmines. Brick walls enclose the pool area and support a raised bed of roses with a backdrop of burning bush. Climbing hydrangea clings to brick pillars around the feet of a bronze lad as if to anchor him to the earth.

Behind the pool house is a shaded service patio of brick with a huge outdoor grill for large parties. A formal circular, tiered

The pool house is the focus for summer activities.

A Japanese maple and gooseneck loosestrife make a showy entrance to the woodland garden.

fountain is ringed with mound-shaped boxwoods and enveloped with a bed of hostas and ferns sweeping back to the nearby woods.

You can slip through an opening in a hedge that isolates the service patio to find the entrance to a woodland garden, nestled under a canopy of mature maples and a few black walnuts. The understory is enriched with plants with interesting foliage—Japanese maples, rhododendrons, and leatherleaf viburnums. A mulched path circles beneath graceful overhead boughs through the woods.

The walk passes a rustic twig bench with curving topline, a naturalistic water garden, and informal clusters of hostas, bleeding hearts, and hardy geraniums. Wild ginger and purple-leaved coralbells spread beneath the upright plumes of lady fern. Spotted silver leaves of lungwort form creeping clumps nearby. Hardy begonias cluster amid foamflower and wintercreeper euonymous. Aggressive gooseneck loosestrife is in there too, its spread tempered by the thick maple roots and shady site.

The remaining garden room spreads from the back of the property to the front of the house. It is dominated by a spacious lawn and edged in an attractive mixed border that includes red-leaved Japanese maples, purple smokebushes, pink-flowered 'The Fairy' roses, azaleas, and ferns. A bottlebrush buckeye spreads beneath a large crabapple, grouped with a red-leaved Japanese maple, red-berried English holly, and daylilies.

These gardens invite strolling visitors to watch the foliage and flowers change throughout the seasons. With splashing water, wind chimes, and fragrant flowers, they appeal to the ears and nose as well as the eyes, which is part of their charm.

Aesthetic Transitions

When designing a series of garden rooms, each with different character, Freeman creates subtle transition zones in between, using finesse and artistry to lead from one garden to the next.

At one Ladue, Missouri, property, Freeman has designed a natural, nearly wild poolside garden, a formal patio and allee, and a sprightly cottage garden, each with a unique atmosphere.

A splashing fountain adds life to the service patio.

Behind the house is a formal brick patio, enclosed by a low brick wall and centered on a small fountain—a cherub in a tiny pool encircled by a bed of variegated myrtle. An allee, created between two rows of crabapples, spreads deep into the lawn to a gazebo surrounded by shade trees.

To the left, the garden grows wilder as beds change from formal geometric patterns to more naturalistic blends of azaleas mingled with clusters of hosta, ferns, and periwinkle.

Beyond a wrought-iron gate in a corner of the property, the transition to wild garden is made complete. The wild garden is

Above: A brick patio overlooks a cheerful cottage garden.

Right: A naturalistic pool fills a quiet shade garden.

dominated by a free-form swimming pool, with rock-clad banks and submerged boulders, all designed in the image of a woodland pond. It is surrounded by a terrace of bluestone and red sandstone, colors highlighted by nearby red-leaf Japanese maples and blue-leaved hostas, tempered with a rich background of greenery.

"Color is incredibly important to me," Freeman says. "This garden sings color, and there are no blossoms in it at all, the interest coming from greens, bronzes, glaucous blues, and intriguing foliage textures."

Above: Off the formal patio is a crabapple allee.

Below: A potpourri of different annual and perennial flowers fills the informal cottage garden.

Changes in grade help define different spaces in this garden.

To the right of the formal terrace is a cottage garden of mixed annuals and perennials in geometrically shaped, stone-edged beds that lie below a white picket fence with an undulating top. Bright colors of all sorts come from phlox, candytuft, hardy geraniums, bee balm, and marigolds—a vivid contrast to the pool garden not far behind.

Garden Rooms Without Walls

A landscape need not be carved up with tall walls and hedges to be separated into different functional spaces. Changes in grade or paving material or the use of low walls and hedges can give the feel of separation without the isolation that comes from complete enclosure.

The bluestone terrace is decked out for swimming and entertaining.

One St. Louis–area landscape by Freeman provides a perfect example. It is a stunning design, with a pool, hot tub, putting green, formal rose garden, and herbal cutting garden, as well as mixed borders that blend it all together. A two-story white gazebo and porch stretch across the rear of the spacious brick home, creating a transition between the house and garden. The white theme is repeated throughout the garden with white wicker furniture and white stone statuary.

As a whole, the yard gives an impression of informal elegance with blended, asymmetrical clusters of trees and shrubs and drifts of flowers that appear to be naturalized. But there are changes of ambiance within each space that gives each a separate personality.

The front yard is spacious and includes a cunningly camouflaged golf tee hidden on a natural-looking grassy rise. The most dynamic portion of the landscape lies in the back yard. A wide, gracious bluestone terrace, inset with red sandstone, surrounds the swimming pool, rock-banked hot tub, and other patio furnishings.

The terrace area is edged in a colorful mixed border that separates it from the rear of the yard, without walling it in completely. For this cheerful screen, Freeman used blue spruce and white pine, red-leaved Japanese maples, hydrangeas, and false cypress, plus ornamental grasses, peonies, pansies, snapdragons, and other annuals. Behind the screen, in what appears to be a quiet patch of lawn, is the putting green, where tees from other parts of the lawn converge.

Beside the terrace, bluestone walks sweep along the house, dropping down a graceful set of arcing bluestone stairs to a formal rose garden enclosed in a low stone retaining wall. Unlike the more informal curves used for the other beds, this rose garden has a classic sundial configuration. Eight wedged-shaped plantings are each devoted to a different color of rose. Behind the rose garden lie tennis courts edged in a European hornbeam hedge, designed to shelter players from the wind.

Another walk veers closer to the house, up a white-railed stair to the gazebo and a raised herb garden that is perched atop a dry-stone retaining wall.

While it is easy to see that these different gardens are part of the same grand plan, each has its own personality and purpose. While used here in a larger property, the same ideas will work nicely in a smaller yard, where a large hedge or fence would seem overwhelming.

A network of balconies and an elevated gazebo allow enjoyment of the garden from above.

Eleven

ELEGANT WORKING GARDENS

or Midwestern pioneers, working the soil was a necessary part of life. For the current generation, it has become an important part of life as well—less from necessity than from the sheer earthly joy and tactile pleasure of the gardening experience and the rewards of the harvest.

The scent of tomato foliage, rubbed as the fruit is plucked; the blue gleam of broccoli and cabbage

Broccoli, basil, and onions thrive in Vicki Nowicki's kitchen garden.

plants as pretty as any glaucous conifer; and the rambunctious vigor of a vining bean twining up a trellis are impressions that transcend the years. Like stroking the fine fur of a calico cat, the sheer physical enjoyment is a primordial pleasure and a respite from an electronically driven world.

There are many choices open to those who like to grow their own herbs and vegetables. Parsley, lettuce, arugula, peas, broccoli, cabbage, and brussels sprouts thrive during the cool spring and fall growing seasons. Tomatoes, squash, cucumbers, beans, basil, and corn make the most of the summer.

Working gardens require an intimate interaction between gardener and garden to ensure that crops reach their full potential. But for every weed pulled or every tomato staked, there is an immediate reward and a promise of good things to come.

A working garden can offer additional benefits as well. It can charm the eye with varying hues of succulent greenery, especially when planted with attractive structure and design.

While the classic Midwestern working garden has long rows of corn and beans, designed to allow tilling in the spaces between the rows, change is in the air. The European concept of the kitchen garden, a productive and beautiful plot blending vegetables, herbs, flowers, walks, walls, and other structures, is making inroads in the Midwest. Some garden designers are stepping into this arena, crafting gardens that are visually enticing as well as productive and useful.

In this chapter you will meet two herb nurserywomen and designers—Libby Bruch, maker of a classic knot garden in Wooster, Ohio, and arLene Shannon of Shipshewana, Indiana, with her herbal four-square garden. You'll also learn about a distinctive approach to vegetable gardening used by Vicki Nowicki of Downers Grove, Illinois.

A Classic Herb Garden

Herbs, with their fragrant and flavorful foliage, have been grown almost since the dawning of civilization. Used for medicine, seasonings, dyes, aroma, and household products, they were essentials in

Pungent-rooted variegated horseradish has white-marbled leaves.

early physic gardens, kitchen gardens, and cottage gardens. Today herbs may be woven into existing landscape beds—for instance, by letting bush basil mingle with petunias or allowing thyme to spread between flagstone steps. Herbs also can be set into a formal or informal garden of their own.

One of the most dramatic centerpieces for an herb garden is an herbal knot, a feature from Elizabethan England. Ribbons of herbal foliage of different colors are interlaced to form attractive geometric patterns that make an intriguing focal point for a garden. Libby Bruch, designer and nurserywoman at Quailcrest Farm in Wooster, Ohio, with the help of her son, Toby, devised a formal herb garden using an eye-catching combination of teucrium, red barberry, and green santolina.

The knot occupies the center of a brick terrace inset with rectangular beds of herbs and enclosed by a brown picket fence, low wall of old barn foundation stones, and short hedge of lavender. Mints contained in large terra-cotta drain tiles flank the fence, along with old-fashioned roses. At both ends of the garden, wooden benches rest under wooden pergolas draped in climbing roses and autumn-blooming clematis.

A knot garden of interwoven foliage forms the focal point of Libby Bruch's Quailcrest Farm herb garden.

Old-fashioned shrub roses add fragrance to the late-spring herb garden. Their buds and petals can be dried for potpourri.

The knot garden is framed with a rectangular edging of germander, with aromatic, dark green, glossy, toothed leaves. Because germander, like many herbs, has an informal and irregular shape, Bruch keeps it sheared into a boxy miniature hedge.

Inside these enclosing arms of germander, red and green herbs flare out around an intricate stone sundial, carving mirror-image lines and appearing to slip under one another where they meet and cross. The green strand is made of clipped fine-leaved, fragrant green santolina while the contrasting red is 'Crimson Pygmy' barberry, which grows only a foot high and requires little shearing.

All three plants have been selected for their reliable hardiness, an important factor in this Zone 5 climate. Excessive winter dieback of slightly tender plants—such as gray santolina—can disfigure the knot for weeks or months, until new growth fills in to make a solid line. Although Bruch avoids gray santolina, she has seen it work well in the lower Midwest, where winter cold is not as severe.

Walkways of weathered brick divide herb beds.

This garden is strengthened by dramatic hardscape. One of the boldest elements is the sundial. Adding sculpture such as this, says Bruch, is an easy and elegant way to give the garden a focus. Other hardscape options include birdbaths, statues, stone containers, and handsome terra-cotta pots filled with flowers and foliage.

Above: Lemon thyme, with citrus-scented foliage, is covered with petite flowers in late spring.

Below: The milky sap of the mole plant is thought to keep moles from tunneling nearby.

Beyond the knot, paths are important for the appearance and function of the garden. Bruch's terrace walkways are made of old brick, with a weathered patina that harmonizes with herbs and gives a feeling of antiquity to the garden. But bricks are not easy to maintain over the decades. They will begin to shift in the earth and eventually will require resetting.

The other herbal beds are more informally planted. Each showcases a different type of herb. One is devoted to popular scented geraniums—rose, lemon, nutmeg, and others. Another is filled with various thymes, such as variegated lemon, camphor, 'Archer's Gold', and white moss, each plant separated by a brick barrier. A trial garden mixes various types of oregano, basil, marjoram, lavender, dill, parsley, and rosemary. A garden of herbal oddities includes a mole plant, with a milky sap thought to send moles fleeing; a chaste tree, with fragrant palmate foliage and lilac-blue flowers; and giant burnet, with flowers that look like bottle-scrubbers. Unusual and interesting but tender herbs also are included.

The garden enclosures, while not tall enough to isolate the herb garden from the surrounding property, give this garden a personality of its own, unfettered by other gardens nearby. In addition to a picket fence, stone wall, or lavender hedge, you can enclose an herb garden with a split-rail fence, which allows the sun to shine through and is ideal for a colonial-style herb garden. Bruch also suggests an evergreen hedge of hardy boxwood such as 'Vardar Valley' or 'Glencoe' or fast-growing arborvitae.

Libby Bruch takes a break with her dog, Cassidy.

Making Herbs a Family Affair

A love of herbs, perennials, roses, and gardens has led Libby Bruch to create a charming country nursery with twenty-four display gardens on a picturesque ridge near Wooster, Ohio. Bruch inherited her love of gardening from her mother and has passed it down to her children—Toby, who runs the herb division and maintains the herb garden; Ginna Bruch Phillips, who handles roses and perennials; Rusty, who focuses on landscape design and shrubs; and Deborah, who manages the gift shops.

The 200-acre property was a working dairy farm when Bruch planted her first field of bare-root perennials in 1975. While the nursery still sells a few field-grown perennials, it also has state-of-the-art greenhouses, a pottery room, gift shops, and a vintage schoolhouse with a small, old-fashioned herb garden.

When it comes to design, Bruch encourages gardeners to take a firm hand in development of their own gardens.

"Too many people don't trust their own judgment," Bruch says. "They end up doing what everyone else is doing and following boring standards. It's better to get a good book on herb-garden design from the library, look through and find a style you like, then work to make it your own."

Bruch teaches basics such as which low-growing herbs should be in the front of the garden and which taller herbs are more appro-

Seven-foot-high angelica stands tall beside a shop wall.

priate in the rear. The low-growing tier may include thymes, dianthus, winter savory, Canada ginger, dwarf germander, and ornamental rock roses. In the mid-border you might find red-stemmed ruby chard, lavender, oregano, rosemary, and lemon verbena. In the rear are the tallest herbs—Russian sage, lovage, angelica, 'Coronation Gold' yarrow, and anise hyssop. A background planting often includes large shrubs such as winterberry holly and shrub roses such as 'The Fairy', 'Nearly Wild', and 'Carefree Beauty'.

For warm-season growing, Bruch recommends cutting-grown 'Aussie Sweet' basil, which sets no seed and needs no deadheading, and 'African Blue', a strongly fragrant basil with purple stems and showy flower spikes.

Bruch believes that members of the artemisia clan are particularly good minglers. The silver foliage of hardy 'Hunington's Garden' looks good beside perennial flowers of blue and pink. Citrus-scented, insect-repelling southernwood is a big, shrubby plant for a large perennial border or large herb garden. Sweet Annie artemisia, a self-seeding annual, turns golden in fall and fills fading gardens with color.

Valerian, with sweetly scented white flowers, arises in many of Bruch's gardens from self-sown seed. It intertwines with crimson barberries beside a water garden, stands amid a profusion of

Fragrant-flowered valerian grows behind 'Silver Queen' artemisia.

Tea mint is contained between brick walks.

artemisia in a perennial garden, and makes a large thicket surrounding a floral mailbox, providing an element of familiarity linking all of these spaces.

While good looks are important for ornamental herbs, easy accessibility is vital for culinary herbs. Bruch keeps all of her favorite kitchen herbs in a garden bed between two brick walks near the kitchen door. The walks' wedge formation entraps aggressively creeping tea mint, which otherwise might escape and spread through any open soil nearby. Culinary herbs—lovage, 'Berggarten' sage, parsley, bush basil, sweet basil, purple basil, French tarragon, rosemary, Greek oregano, lemon thyme, garlic chives, lemon verbena, and self-seeding dill—make a useful and informal culinary garden.

Along the foundation of Bruch's historic house and beside pristine white cellar doors, herbs mingle with decoratives in a charming scene. 'Munstead' lavender, a miniature rose, baby's breath, golden lemon thyme, white moss thyme, silver thyme, and woolly thyme replace the usual foundation planting.

Having gardened in northeast Ohio for forty-five years, Bruch has learned to accept everything the weather brings with a shrug.

"You learn to be realistic," she says. "Everyone would love it if it would rain once a week on Sunday night and be sunny for the rest of the week, but that's not how it works around here."

She's learned to plan for weather's worst. To keep soil from becoming over-soaked during heavy rains, she recommends raised beds. To keep plants growing during drought, she relies on irrigation and extensive mulching.

"You can't lose if you are well prepared," she says.

Doorside Herbs

In Shipshewana, a quiet village in the heart of Indiana's Amish country, life moves at a leisurely pace, as horse-drawn buggies and hand-cut hay set the tone. Once the warm season arrives, however, a mammoth outdoor flea market opens on Tuesdays and Wednesdays, attracting 50,000 tourists a week and congesting area roads. In the midst of these contrasting worlds lies a small but beau-

'New Dawn', trained on a Quailcrest pergola, is one of the most reliable climbing roses for northeast Ohio.

tiful array of herb gardens at Greenfield Herb Garden, a nursery and herb shop.

Greenfield Herb Garden, located on a side street in the heart of Shipshewana, includes a rustic-looking building clad in weathered barn siding with jaunty red window frames and flashings. The quarter-acre tract also includes two large gardens of field-grown herbs and about a dozen display gardens, including a charming modified four-square garden designed by owner arLene Shannon.

A wrought-iron hoop fence made by the local blacksmith encloses the four-square garden. In a narrow strip between the fence and the front sidewalk stretches a lawn of mixed thymes, a thick carpet of fragrant greenery. In a large opening against the shop wall, Shannon has trained two espaliered apple trees, pruned into a single plane to show the geometric pattern of their carefully planned branching. Arcing over a protruding bay window nearby is a rambling, pink-flowered sweet briar rose, a prolific late spring bloomer with fragrant foliage.

Within these boundaries the formal, patterned herb garden has beautiful simplicity. The garden beds are arranged in four stylized, timber-edged raised planting areas around a central diamond-shaped bed. The walks

Patterned raised beds divided by brick-chip walks give this herb garden distinction.

Wrought-iron hoops make an herb garden enclosure.

MORE VARIATIONS ON
THE FOUR-SQUARE LAYOUT

Ken Miller has designed this more formal kitchen garden.

Both Cliff Miller of Lake Bluff, Illinois, and Ken Miller of St. Louis—who are related only in their love of gardens—design working gardens that follow the four-square theme.

One of Ken Miller's clients has a kitchen garden of vegetables and herbs at the entryway to the back yard, a prelude to the entertaining area and perennial garden. A white wooden fence surrounds the garden while a brick path runs along the perimeter of the four-square, dividing it from a rectangular edging bed. Four beds surround a central sundial and are further defined with an edging of low, clipped boxwood hedges. Narrow, informal brick paths separate the beds and provide the gardener with access.

Herbs and vegetables share beds—rosemary and thyme with peppers, sage with zucchini, and asparagus underplanted with cucumber vines. Single-stemmed tomatoes climb spiraling supports, against a backdrop of pink climbing roses on a white fence.

Cliff Miller's clients have converted a cut-flower garden in an opening in their wooded lot into a kitchen garden. Four rectangular beds, edged on the inside with a circular hedge of boxwood, surround a

From Farm Market to Herb Garden

ArLene Shannon is a teacher-turned-gardener, lured into the herb business after spending her summers growing herbs to sell at a Chicago farm market.

"People were amazed at the variety of herbs I offered beyond basic parsley. I also started drying flowers and making herbal crafts, potpourris, and wreaths. I soon found I was having more fun with this than with teaching," Shannon says.

At Greenfield Herb Garden in Shipshewana, she grows over 400 varieties of herbs, including out-of-the-ordinary plants like non-blooming lamb's ears, dwarf meadowsweet, variegated horseradish, hardy 'Woodcote' golden sage, and lavender mint.

In addition to the four-square garden, Shannon displays miniature gardens such as a chocolate garden with 'Chocolate Veil' purple-leaved coralbells, chocolate mint, chocolate-mint scented geraniums, and a cocoa-bean mulch. An herbal tea garden has bronze fennel, alpine strawberries, German chamomile, lemon verbena, black-stem peppermint, and lemon thyme enveloping a large iron tea kettle. Shannon also has designed

ArLene Shannon works in her nursery beds.

A miniature faerie garden illustrates how to use herbs in an informal design.

herb gardens for the Mennonite Center in Shipshewana and other local properties.

"Herbs have given me a sense of serenity in my life. I enjoy walking in the garden. It is calming. But I also know that these herbs will serve me in many ways, a source of satisfaction. It's thrifty and functional, which appeals to my Midwestern rural ethic," Shannon says.

STYLISH HERBS

If you want herbs that look great in the garden, consider the following recommendations from arLene Shannon of Greenfield Herb Garden.

- Basil comes in mounded or vase shapes, with leaves that vary from miniature to lettuce leaf, in colors of green and purple.

- Sage lends itself to groupings for bold clusters or sweeps of color. You can choose from silver, golden variegated, purple, and tricolor types.

- Onions have a distinctive upright form, attractive flowers, and interesting seed heads. They also mix well with creeping and mound-shaped herbs. Try a variety, including Welsh onions, chives, Egyptian walking onions, and garlic chives.

- Trailing nasturtiums, old-fashioned vines with bright orange, edible flowers, have a loose, natural shape beautiful for cascading over tree stumps, along garden paths, and out of baskets.

- Thymes, alone or in mixtures, are handsome for spreading in any low, flat space, including along a hot, dry driveway edge where few other plants will thrive.

- Catmints, with distinctive and fragrant silver-green leaves, have a loose, open, sometimes sprawling form, ideal for an informal garden. Blue flowers arrive in late spring, and if cut back, will bloom again in summer.

If there is one secret to success with herbs, Shannon says, it's to keep the herb garden close to home.

"If the herbs are within ten feet of the kitchen door, you'll use them," she says. "If they are within twenty feet, you'll talk about them. If over twenty feet away, you'll only look at them."

A Vegetable Garden with Pizzazz

Vicki Nowicki's kitchen garden in Downers Grove, Illinois, is a place for teaching and social gatherings as well as harvesting. The garden, which takes up an 85- by 88-foot back yard, is surrounded by an evergreen windbreak and a wood-land garden of native plants. Although the kitchen garden began as an ordinary vegetable garden, it wasn't long before Nowicki began to experiment with different layouts, looking for one that was efficient, easy to use, and attractive.

Nowicki decided to adopt a more "organic" shape that incorporated raised garden beds.

Meandering straw paths wind between arcing beds, all of which

In this garden sweet peas and cosmos for bouquets mingle with culinary vegetables and herbs.

The design strength of paths and bed lines becomes clear when viewed from above.

Above: Basils mix with salvias and roses near the house.

Below: A bed of onions and Swiss chard encircles a central butterfly garden.

are less than four feet wide and can be worked from the side without stepping in the organically rich soil. In the center of the vegetable garden is a butterfly garden, with purple coneflowers, verbena, and butterfly bushes. Dragonflies, bats, and even a screech owl live near the garden, eating pests before they can plague the plants.

"I don't have to get in my car and drive somewhere to find a connection with the natural world. I can begin to make that connection right here in my own yard, even in the vegetable garden," Nowicki says.

Bold sentinels stand at the garden entrance— 'Thérèse Bugnet' rose, catmint, peonies, Dame's rocket, and bold-leaved 'Victoria', 'Valentine', and an unnamed heirloom rhubarb—drawing visitors into the garden. Vegetables, herbs, and flowers are not planted in rows but are given free-form blocks of open space, growing shoulder to shoulder with their neighbors. This kind of interplanting makes maximum use of garden space, helps to hold moisture and to shade out weeds, and provides beautiful blends of foliage and flowers.

'Baby Blanket' ground cover roses mix with carrots, 'Siam Queen' basil, parsley, and parcel, an herb that combines the flavor and appearance of celery and parsley. Garlic stands amid redstemmed Swiss chard. Young tomato plants blend with spring lettuce, arugula, and early green beans. Nowicki thins out the lettuce and arugula as summer progresses, leaving more room for the beans and tomatoes to spread out. Radishes and spinach are interplanted next to a swirl of shallots.

There is method to this madness, as waves of different crops suited to alternating cool and warm seasons fill the beds with an endless succession of produce.

An entryway arbor adds elegance to this working garden.

"Vegetables are planted in balanced patterns and, as they are harvested and spaces open up, the spaces become part of the patterns," Nowicki says. "Just use seed or transplants to fill open areas, and the new crops, bolstered by the colors of the annual flowers, will fit right in and create a new pattern."

In the rear of the garden, a hillside planting includes dwarf fruit trees and hills of pumpkins and squash that trail down the slope. 'Six Hills Giant' catmint blends with asparagus near clusters of maiden grass, fountain grass, switch grass, and 'Othello' roses. In small openings here and there, Nowicki tucks in potatoes, pole beans, cucumber towers, lilies, 'Rocket' snapdragons, and 'State Fair' zinnias for cutting.

"I try to use everything that's out there, even the volunteer weeds," Nowicki says. "I harvest dandelions and violets to make into jelly. This self-reliant behavior keeps us out of the fast-paced loop of life today."

Gardening As a Lifestyle

Garden designer Vicki Nowicki loves the sensory pleasures of gardening.

Vicki Nowicki, who has a master's degree in environmental education and interpretive services, worked at the Brookfield Zoo near Chicago for eight years, then freelanced in the same field around the country before settling down to garden designing. It was in the mid-1980s when Nowicki went into business with her husband, Ron Nowicki, a landscape architect who designs native and naturalistic landscapes.

The pair divide their design and installation tasks. He installs hardscape, trees, shrubs, and lighting while Vicki works with flowers, herbs, and gardens for butterflies and birds.

"For me, garden designing is a more intellectual process. But it's the gardening itself, the outdoor life among the smells, and colors, and sounds of the garden that bring me back down from intellect simply into my senses. This is the ultimate way to appreciate your surroundings and to fully live," she says.

Nowicki believes that it is essential to live simply. She enriches her life by minimizing energy use and growing her own food.

"The more vegetables we grow, the more we like it," Nowicki says.

To make the garden grow its best, Nowicki uses every trick in the book—and some new ones of her own, which she teaches in classes at the Chicago Botanic Garden and Morton Arboretum.

To plant blocks of seeds, Nowicki uses an old-fashioned four-pointed dibble, with pencil-like prongs that make a grid of equidistant holes in the soil. It works particularly well with large-seeded vegetables, such as beans, peas, beets, rutabagas, and corn, as well as small onion sets. It's fast and easy and allows you to plant clusters of vegetables amid other plants, using every inch of space.

Nowicki buys inexpensive packages of quick-growing radish seeds to use as garden markers. She sprinkles them amid the slow-starting seeds of parsnips so the early emerging radish leaves can mark the spot.

Carrots, which also are slow to germinate, may not sprout at all if the soil surface bakes into a crust in the sun. By sowing the carrots with radishes, Nowicki uses the radishes to break up the soil surface for the carrot seedlings that follow. She mixes a 1:1 blend of carrot and radish seeds for a 3- by 4-foot bed of fine, prepared soil. She sprinkles half of the seeds lightly over the bed, easily seeing where the large radish seeds have fallen. With the remaining half of the seed mix, she fills in areas that are bare. She then covers the seeds with compost and pats it down. As the radishes grow, she pulls them out, making extra space for the carrots to expand and eliminating the need for thinning and weeding.

For an easy harvest of potatoes, Nowicki lays potatoes on the ground and covers them with 12 to 16 inches of straw. The tubers sprout in the straw, which can be brushed away when the potatoes are ready to be harvested.

Leeks are started in a foot-deep trench. As the stems grow tall, Nowicki pushes the soil around the base to blanch and sweeten them.

Sweet and hot peppers are planted in large tin tubs, which stay warmer than the surrounding soil and allow peppers to grow and mature more quickly.

Nowicki recycles everything possible from in and around the garden. A cucumber trellis is fashioned out of cuttings from an apple tree. Most of the compost used to enrich the soil is made from the previous seasons' fallen leaves and garden scraps.

"Gardening is a way to connect artfulness to a direct experience of nature," Nowicki says. "It's a way to give back to the earth some of the joy and abundance that we have been given."

Peppers, which thrive in warm weather, mature most quickly when grown in tubs.

EPILOGUE

learly, there is more to the Midwest than corn and soybeans. We have abundant kitchen gardens that could rival any French potager, and magnificent estate gardens as handsome as their classic British counterparts. We have gardens that celebrate woodland and prairie resources unique to the region. And evergreens brighten winter landscapes, as perennials nestled below the ground make the most of our robust seasons.

But the greatest Midwestern hurrah comes from our garden designers—talented individuals able to turn ordinary spaces into living art. They make the outdoor world a wonderful place in which to rest, relax, and connect with nature and are enhancing the region, garden by garden.

APPENDIX

DESIGNER CONTACTS

Craig Bergmann Landscape Design, Inc.
1924 Lake Avenue
Wilmette, IL 60091
847-251-8355

Charles W. Freeman, Inc.
1305 Baur Boulevard
St. Louis, Missouri 63132
314-993-9010

Douglas Hoerr Landscape Architecture, Inc.
1330 Sherman Avenue
Evanston, IL 60201
847-733-0140

Girard Nurseries
6839 North Ridge Road
Geneva, OH 44041
440-466-2881

Greenfield Herb Garden
PO Box 9
Shipshewana, IN 46565
219-768-7110

Horticultural Associates, Inc.
PO Box 301
Gurnee, IL 60031-0301
847-662-7475

June Hutson
Missouri Botanical Garden Kemper Center
4344 Shaw Boulevard
St. Louis, MO 63166
314-577-5100

Ken Miller Horticultural Consultants
113 West Argonne
Kirkwood, MO 63122-8073
314-966-4644

The Land Office
907 Summit Street
Downers Grove, IL 60515
630-852-5263

P. Clifford Miller, Inc.
11 North Skokie Highway, Suite 200
Lake Bluff, IL 60044
847-234-6664

Brian Parsons
Holden Arboretum
9500 Sperry Road
Kirtland, OH 44094-5172
440-946-4400

The Pattie Group, Inc.
15533 Chillicothe Road
Novelty, OH 44072
440-338-1288

Prairie Sun Consultants
612 Staunton Road
Naperville, IL 60565
630-983-8404

Quailcrest Farm
2801 Armstrong Road
Wooster, OH 44691
330-345-6722

Rich's Foxwillow Pines Nursery
11618 McConnell Road
Woodstock, IL 60098
815-338-7442

Jane Rogers
Cantigny Gardens and Museums
1 South 151 Winfield Road
Wheaton, IL 60187
630-260-8169

Savanna Designs
3511 Lake Elmo Avenue North
Lake Elmo, MN 55042
612-770-6910

PROFESSIONAL LANDSCAPE ORGANIZATIONS

Association of Professional Landscape Designers
104 South Michigan Avenue,
    Suite 1500
Chicago, IL 60603
312-201-0101

American Society of Landscape Architects
4401 Connecticut Avenue NW,
    5th Floor
Washington D.C. 20008
202-686-2752

American Nursery and Landscape Association
1250 Eye Street NW, Suite 500
Washington D.C. 20005
202-789-2900

Illinois Landscape Contractors Association
2200 South Main Street, Suite 304
Lombard, IL 60148-5366
630-932-8443

Illinois Nurserymen's Association
1717 South Fifth Street
Springfield, IL 62703-3116
217-525-6222

Indiana Association of Nurserymen
11595 North Meridian Street,
    Suite 300
Carmel, IN 46032
800-443-7336

Kansas Association of Nurserymen
411 Poplar
Wamego, KS 66547-1446
913-456-8338

Michigan Nursery and Landscape Association
2149 Commons Parkway
Okemos, MI 48864
517-381-0437

Minnesota Nursery and Landscape Association
2151 Hamline Avenue North,
    Suite 109
St. Paul, MN 55113-0003
612-633-4987

Ohio Nursery and Landscape Association
72 Dorchester Square
Westerville, OH 43081-3350
614-899-1195

Oklahoma State Nurserymen's Association
400 North Portland Street
Oklahoma City, OK 73107-6110
405-942-5276

South Dakota Nursery and Landscape Association
East River Nursery
RR 5, Box 392A
Huron, SD 57350-8842
605-352-4414

Wisconsin Nursery Association, Inc.
9910 West Layton
Greenfield, WI 53228-3347
414-529-4705

SOME MIDWESTERN NURSERIES

Arrowhead Alpines
PO Box 857
Fowlerville MI 48836
517-223-3581
(mail order)

Busse Gardens
5873 Oliver Avenue SW
Cokato, MN 55321-4229
320-286-5445
(mail order, display gardens)

Carolee's Herb Farm
3305 South 100 West
Hartford City, IN 47348
765-348-3162
(display gardens)

Craig Bergmann's Country Garden
700 Kenosha Road
Winthrop Harbor, IL 60096-0424
847-746-0311
(display gardens)

Crystal Palace Perennials
12029 Wicker Avenue
Cedar Lake, IN 46303
219-374-9419
(mail order, display garden, aquatic
    plants)

Girard Nurseries
6839 North Ridge Road
Geneva, OH 44041
440-466-2881
(mail order, display gardens)

Greenfield Herb Garden
PO Box 9
Shipshewana, IN 46565
219-768-7110
(display gardens)

Klehm Nursery
4210 North Duncan Road
Champaign, IL 61821
800-553-3715
(mail order)

Milaeger's Gardens
4838 Douglas Avenue
Racine, WI 53402-2498
800-669-9956
(mail order, display gardens)

Prairie Nursery
PO Box 306
Westfield, WI 53964
608-296-3679
(mail order)

Quailcrest Farm
2801 Armstrong Road
Wooster, OH 44691
330-345-6722
(display gardens)

Rich's Foxwillow Pines Nursery
11618 McConnell Road
Woodstock, IL 60098
815-338-7442
(mail order, display gardens)

Shady Oaks Nursery
112 10th Avenue SE
Waseca, MN 56093
800-504-8006
(mail order, display gardens)

Stream Cliff Herb Farm
8225 South County Road 90 West
Commiskey, IN 47227
812-346-5859
(display gardens)

Wade and Gatton Nurseries
1288 Gatton Rocks Road
Bellville, OH 44813-9106
419-883-3191
(mail order, display gardens)

SOME PUBLIC GARDENS

Bicklehaupt Arboretum
340 South 14th Street
Clinton, IA 52723-5432
319-242-4771

Boerner Botanical Garden
5879 South 92nd Street
Hales Corners, WI 53130
414-425-1130

Cantigny Gardens and Museums
1 South 151 Winfield Road
Wheaton, IL 60187
630-668-5161

Chicago Botanic Garden
1000 Lake Cook Road
Glencoe, IL 60022-0400
847-835-8366

Cleveland Botanical Garden
11030 East Boulevard
Cleveland, OH 44106
216-721-1600

Dawes Arboretum
7770 Jacksontown Road SE
Newark, OH 43056
740-323-2990

Des Moines Botanical Center
909 East River Drive
Des Moines, IA 50316
515-242-2934

Fellows Riverside Gardens
816 Glenwood Avenue
Youngstown, OH 44502
330-740-7116

Fernwood
13988 Range Line Road
Niles, MI 49120
616-695-6491

Holden Arboretum
9500 Sperry Road
Kirtland, OH 44094-5172
440-946-4400

Indianapolis Museum of Art Botanical Garden
1200 West 38th Street
Indianapolis, IN 46208
317-923-1331

Kingwood Center
900 Park Avenue West
Mansfield, OH 44906
419-522-0211

Minnesota Landscape Arboretum
3675 Arboretum Drive
Chanhassen, MN 55317
612-443-2460

Missouri Botanical Garden
4344 Shaw Boulevard
St. Louis, MO 63166
314-577-5100

Morton Arboretum
4100 Illinois Route 53
Lisle, IL 60532-1293
630-968-0074

Toledo Botanical Garden
5403 Elmer Drive
Toledo, OH 43615
419-936-2986

REGIONAL MAGAZINES

Chicagoland Gardening
PO Box 208
Downers Grove, IL 60515-0208

The Weedpatch Gazette
PO Box 339
Richmond, IL 60071-0339

A LIST OF COMMON NAMES

෨

Note: *Hortus III* (1976: Macmillan Publishing, New York, NY) has been used as a primary nomenclature reference with some more recent synonyms added. According to botanical tradition, all specific epithets are lower case. The use of spp. refers to multiple species within the genus.

A

Aaron's-beard (*Hypericum kalmianum*)
ageratum (*Ageratum houstonianum*)
amur honeysuckle (*Lonicera maackii*)
angelica or archangel (*Angelica archangelica*)
anise hyssop (*Agastache foeniculum*)
arborvitae (*Thuja* spp.)
aromatic aster (*Aster oblongifolius*)
arrowwood viburnum (*Viburnum dentatum*)
arugula (*Eruca vesicaria*)
artemisia (*Artemisia* spp.)
aster (*Aster* spp.)
astilbe (*Astilbe* spp.)
autumn-blooming or sweet autumn clematis (*Clematis paniculata* syn. *C. terniflora*)

B

baby-blue-eyes (*Nemophila menziesii*)
baby's-breath (*Gypsophila paniculata*, *G. repens*, *G. elegans*)
bachelor's-button (*Centaurea cyanus*)
bald cypress (*Taxodium distichum*)
balloon flower (*Platycodon grandiflorus*)
baptisia (*Baptisia* spp.)
barberry (*Berberis* spp.)
beard-tongue (*Penstemon* spp.)
bear's-breech (*Acanthus mollis*)
bee balm (*Monarda* spp.)
beech (*Fagus* spp.)
bellflower (*Campanula* spp.)
bellwort (*Uvularia grandiflora*)
bergamot (*Monarda* spp.)

betony (*Stachys officinalis*)
bird's-nest spruce (*Picea abies* 'Nidiformis')
big bluestem (*Andropogon gerardii*)
big-leaved aster (*Aster macrophyllus*)
bitter orange (*Poncirus trifoliata*)
black-eyed Susan (*Rudbeckia hirta*)
black locust (*Robinia pseudoacacia*)
black snakeroot (*Cimicifuga racemosa*)
black walnut (*Juglans nigra*)
Blackie sweet-potato vine (*Ipomoea batatas* 'Blackie')
blazing-star (*Liatris* spp.)
bleeding heart (*Dicentra* spp.)
bloody cranesbill (*Geranium sanguineum* also var. *striatum* syn. *lancastriense*)
blue cohosh (*Caulophyllum thalictroides*)
bluegrass (*Poa* spp.)
blue mist shrub or bluebeard (*Caryopteris* x *clandonensis*)
blue salvia (*Salvia farinacea*)
Boston fern (*Nephrolepis exaltata* 'Bostoniensis')
bottlebrush buckeye (*Aesculus parviflora*)
boxwood (*Buxus* spp.)
Brazilian verbena or Brazilian vervain (*Verbena bonariensis*)
broad-leaved goldenrod (*Solidago flexicaulis*)
brown-eyed Susan (*Rudbeckia triloba*)
buckthorn (*Rhamnus* spp.)
buffalo grass (*Buchloe dactyloides*)
bugleweed (*Ajuga* spp.)
burning bush (*Euonymus alata*)
bur oak (*Quercus macrocarpa*)

butterfly bush (*Buddleia davidii*)
butterfly weed (*Asclepias tuberosa*)
butternut walnut (*Juglans cinerea*)

C

caladium (*Caladium* x *hortulanum*)
Canada ginger (*Asarum canadense*)
Canada hemlock (*Tsuga canadensis*)
Canada lily (*Lilium canadense*)
Canada mayflower (*Maianthemum canadense*)
Canada thistle (*Cirsium arvense*)
cardinal flower (*Lobelia cardinalis*)
castor bean (*Ricinus communis*)
catmint (*Nepeta* x *faassenii* syn. *N. mussinii*)
celosia (*Celosia* spp.)
chain fern (*Woodwardia* spp.)
chaste tree (*Vitex agnus-castus*)
chervil (*Anthriscus cerefolium*)
chicory (*Cichorium intybus*)
Chinese forget-me-not (*Brunnera macrophylla*)
chives (*Allium schoenoprasum*)
Christmas fern (*Polystichum acrostichoides*)
chrysanthemum (*Dendranthema* spp. syn. *Chrysanthemum* spp.)
cleft phlox (*Phlox bifida*)
cleome (*Cleome hasslerana*)
climbing hydrangea (*Hydrangea petiolaris*)
club moss (*Lycopodium* spp.)
clustered bellflower (*Campanula glomerata*)

coleus (*Coleus* x *hybridus* syn. *Solenostemon scutellarioides*)

Colorado spruce or Colorado blue spruce (*Picea pungens*)

columbine (*Aquilegia* spp.)

comfrey (*Symphytum officinale*)

common oak sedge (*Carex pensylvanica*)

common yarrow (*Achillea millefolium*)

compass plant (*Silphium laciniatum*)

coneflower (*Echinacea* spp.)

contorted filbert (*Corylus avellana* 'Contorta')

coralbells (*Heuchera* spp.)

coreopsis (*Coreopsis* spp.)

Cornelian cherry dogwood (*Cornus mas*)

cosmos (*Cosmos* spp.)

crabapple (*Malus* spp.)

creeping thyme (*Thymus* spp.)

crocus (*Crocus* spp.)

Culver's root (*Veronicastrum virginicum*)

cut-leaf Japanese maple (*Acer palmatum* 'Dissectum', 'Filigree', and more)

D

Dahlberg daisy (*Thymophylla tenuiloba* syn. *Dyssodia tenuiloba*)

daisy fleabane (*Erigeron annuus*)

dandelion (*Taraxacum officinale*)

Dame's rocket (*Hesperis matronalis*)

daphne (*Daphne* x *burkwoodii, D. mezereum, D. cneorum*)

daylily (*Hemerocallis* spp.)

dianthus (*Dianthus* spp.)

dill (*Anethum graveolens*)

dock (*Rumex* spp.)

doll's-eyes (*Actaea pachypoda*)

doublefile viburnum (*Viburnum plicatum* f. *tomentosum*)

Douglas fir (*Pseudotsuga menziesii*)

dusty-miller (*Centaurea cineraria*)

Dutchman's-breeches (*Dicentra cucullaria*)

dwarf crested iris (*Iris cristata*)

E

early buttercup (*Ranunculus fascicularis*)

Egyptian walking onion (*Allium cepa* Proliferum Group)

elderberry (*Sambucus* spp.)

English holly (*Ilex aquifolium*)

English ivy (*Hedera helix*)

English rose (*Rosa* hyb.)

English Yew (*Taxus baccata*)

epimedium (*Epimedium* spp.)

euonymus (*Euonymus* spp.)

European beech (*Fagus sylvatica*)

European ginger (*Asarum europaeum*)

European hornbeam (*Carpinus betulus*)

European larch (*Larix decidua*)

F

fallopia (*Fallopia* spp.)

false cypress (*Chamaecyparis* spp.)

false rue anemone (*Isopyrum biternatum*)

false Solomon's-seal (*Smilacina racemosa*)

false spirea (*Sorbaria sorbifolia*)

fanflower (*Scaevola aemula*)

feather reed grass (*Calamagrostis* x *acutiflora*)

fennel (*Foeniculum vulgare*)

fern-leaf yarrow (*Achillea filipendulina*)

fescue (*Festuca* spp.)

fibrous-rooted begonia (*Begonia* x *semperflorens-cultorum*)

fire pink (*Silene virginica*)

fleabane (*Erigeron* spp.)

flowering onion (*Allium* spp.)

flowering raspberry (*Rubus odoratus*)

flowering tobacco (*Nicotiana* spp.)

foamflower (*Tiarella* spp.)

forsythia (*Forsythia* spp.)

fountain grass (*Pennisetum setaceum*)

foxglove (*Digitalis* spp.)

foxglove beard-tongue (*Penstemon digitalis*)

French tarragon (*Artemisia dracunculus*)

fringe tree (*Chionanthus virginicus*)

Froebel spirea (*Spiraea* x *bumalda* 'Froebelii')

fuchsia (*Fuchsia* spp.)

G

galax (*Galax aphylla* syn. *G. urceolata*)

garden forget-me-not (*Myosotis sylvatica*)

German iris (*Iris* x *germanica*)

germander (*Teucrium chamaedrys*)

giant or greateer burnet (*Sanguisorba officinalis*)

giant flowering onion (*Allium giganteum*)

ginseng (*Panax quinquefolius*)

globe thistle (*Echinops ritro*)

golden alyssum (*Alyssum saxatile* syn. *Aurinia saxatilis*)

golden coneflower (*Rudbeckia* spp.)

golden marguerite (*Anthemis tinctoria*)

golden ragwort (*Senecio aureus*)

goldenrod (*Solidago* spp.)

goldenseal (*Hydrastis canadensis*)

golden star grass (*Hypoxis hirsuta*)

golden sweet potato vine (*Ipomoea batatas*)

golden white pine (*Pinus strobus* 'Golden Candles', 'Winter Gold', and other gold-leaf cultivars)

goldthread (*Coptis trifolia* subsp. *groenlandica*)

gooseneck loosestrife (*Lysimachia clethroides*)

grape hyacinth (*Muscari* spp.)

gray dogwood (*Cornus racemosa*)

gray santolina or lavender cotton (*Santolina chamaecyparissus*)

gray-headed coneflower (*Ratibida pinnata*)

great white trillium (*Trillium grandiflorum*)

green-and-gold (*Chrysogonum virginianum*)

green santolina (*Santolina virens*)

H

hardy begonia (*Begonia grandis*)

hardy geranium (*Geranium* spp.)

hardy orchid (*Bletilla striata*)

Harry Lauder's walking stick (*Corylus avellana* 'Contorta')

hawthorn (*Crataegus* spp.)

heliotrope (*Heliotropium arborescens*)

hellebore (*Helleborus* spp.)

hemlock (*Tsuga* spp.)

hen and chicks (*Sempervivum* spp.)

hibiscus (*Hibiscus* spp.)

hickory (*Carya* spp.)

Hicks yew (*Taxus* x *media* 'Hicksii')

Hinoki cypress (*Chamaecyparis obtusa*)

honeylocust (*Gleditsia triacanthos*)

hop hornbeam (*Ostrya* spp.)

horehound (*Marrubium* spp.)

horseradish (*Amoracia rusticana*)

hosta (*Hosta* spp.)

hyacinth (*Hyacinthus orientalis*)

hydrangea (*Hydrangea* spp.)

I–J

impatiens (*Impatiens wallerana*)

intermediate wood fern (*Dryopteris intermedia*)

interrupted fern (*Osmunda claytoniana*)

jack-in-the-pulpit (*Arisaema triphyllum*)

jack pine (*Pinus banksiana*)

Japanese anemone (*Anemone* x *hybrida, A. hupehensis* var. *japonica*)

Japanese barberry (*Berberis thunbergii*)

Japanese honeysuckle (*Lonicera japonica*)

Japanese kerria (*Kerria japonica*)

Japanese maple (*Acer palmatum*, *A. japonicum*)

Japanese painted fern (*Athyrium niponicum* 'Pictum')

Japanese primrose (*Primula japonica*)

Japanese red pine (*Pinus densiflora*)

Japanese spirea (*Spiraea japonica*)

Japanese swamp iris (*Iris kaempferi* syn. *I. ensata*)

Japanese tree lilac (*Syringa reticulata*)

Japanese white pine (*Pinus parviflora*)

jasmine (*Jasminum* spp.)

jewelweed (*Impatiens capensis*, *I. pallida*)

Joe-Pye weed (*Eupatorium purpureum*, *E. maculatum*)

Joseph's coat (*Amaranthus tricolor*)

Judd's viburnum (*Viburnum* x *juddii*)

juniper (*Juniperus* spp.)

K–L

kochia (*Kochia trichophylla*)

kousa dogwood (*Cornus kousa*)

lady fern (*Athyrium filix-femina*)

lady's bedstraw (*Galium* spp.)

lady's-mantle (*Alchemilla mollis*)

lamb's-ears (*Stachys byzantina*)

large cranberry (*Vaccinium macrocarpon*)

larkspur (*Delphinium ajacis* syn. *Consolida ambigua*)

lavender (*Lavandula* spp.)

lavender cotton (*Santolina chamaecyparissus*)

lavender mint (*Mentha* 'Lavender')

lavender thyme (*Thymus vulgaris* 'Wooly-Stemmed Sweet Lavender')

leatherleaf (*Chaemaedaphne calyculata*)

leatherleaf fern or leather wood fern (*Dryopteris marginalis*)

leatherleaf viburnum (*Viburnum rhytidophyllum*)

leatherwood (*Dirca palustris*)

lemon balm (*Melissa officinalis*)

lily-of-the-valley (*Convallaria majalis*)

limber pine (*Pinus flexilis*)

little bluestem (*Schizachyrium scoparium*)

littleleaf linden (*Tilia cordata*)

lousewort (*Pedicularis canadensis*)

lungwort (*Pulmonaria* spp.)

M

magnolia (*Magnolia* spp.)

maiden grass (*Miscanthus* spp.)

maidenhair fern (*Adiantum pedatum*)

maple (*Acer* spp.)

marginal wood fern (*Dryopteris marginalis*)

marigold (*Tagetes* spp.)

marjoram (*Origanum majorana*)

marsh marigold (*Caltha palustris*)

mayapple (*Podophyllum peltatum*)

meadowsweet (*Filipendula* spp.)

Merrill magnolia (*Magnolia* x *loebneri* 'Merrill')

Mexican bamboo (*Polygonum cuspidatum*)

mintleaf (*Plectranthus madagascariensis*)

Mohican viburnum (*Viburnum lantana* 'Mohican')

mole plant (*Euphorbia* spp.)

monkshood (*Aconitum napellus*, *A.* spp.)

Morrow's honeysuckle (*Lonicera morrowii*)

mountain ash (*Sorbus* spp.)

mountain laurel (*Kalmia latifolia*)

mugo pine (*Pinus mugo*)

multiflora rose (*Rosa multiflora*)

myrtle (*Vinca minor*)

N

narrow-leaved glade fern (*Diplazium pycnocarpon* syn. *Athyrium pycnocarpon*)

nasturtium (*Tropaeolum minus*)

nierembergia (*Nierembergia caerulea*)

noble fir (*Abies procera*)

Norway maple (*Acer platanoides*)

Norway spruce (*Picea abies*)

O

oak (*Quercus* spp.)

oakleaf hydrangea (*Hydrangea quercifolia*)

Oconee-bells (*Shortia galacifolia*)

old-fashioned bleeding-heart (*Dicentra spectabilis*)

oleander (*Nerium oleander*)

orange horse gentian (*Triosteum aurantiacum*, *T. perfoliatum*)

oregano or origano (*Origanum vulgare*)

Oriental bittersweet (*Celastrus orbiculatus*)

Oriental lily (*Lilium auratum*, *L. japonicum*, *L. speciosum*, and hybrids)

Oriental poppy (*Papaver orientale*)

Oriental golden spruce (*Picea orientalis* 'Skylands')

ornamental kale (*Brassica oleracea* Acephala Group)

Orris root iris (*Iris* x *germanica* var. *florentina*)

ostrich fern (*Matteuccia pensylvanica*)

P

pachysandra (*Pachysandra* spp.)

pagoda dogwood (*Cornus alternifolia*)

pale purple coneflower (*Echinacea pallida*)

pansy (*Viola* x *wittrockiana*)

paper birch (*Betula papyrifera*)

parsley (*Petroselinium* spp.)

partridgeberry (*Mitchella repens*)

pasqueflower (*Anemone pulsatilla* syn. *Pulsatilla vulgaris*)

pawpaw (*Asimina triloba*)

Pennsylvania sedge (*Carex pensylvanica*)

peony (*Paeonia* spp.)

periwinkle (*Vinca minor*)

Persian fritillary (*Fritillaria persica*)

petunia (*Petunia* x *hybrida*)

pincushion flower (*Scabiosa* spp.)

pink coneflower (*Echinacea pallida*)

pink yarrow (*Achillea millefolium* 'Cerise Queen', hybrid 'Appleblossom', and others)

pin oak (*Quercus palustris*)

pitcher plant (*Sarracenia purpurea*)

plumbago (*Ceratostigma plumbaginoides*)

poppy mallow (*Callirhoe involucrata*)

prairie blazing-star (*Liatris pycnostachya*)

prairie buttercup (*Ranunculus rhomboideus*)

prairie dock (*Silphium terebinthinaceum*)

prairie dropseed (*Sporobolus heterolepis*)

prairie smoke (*Geum triflorum*)

Prairie trillium (*Trillium recurvatum*)

prickly pear cactus (*Opuntia humifusa*)

primrose (*Primula* spp.)

pumpkin ash (*Fraxinus profunda*)

purple coneflower (*Echinacea purpurea*)

pussy-toes (*Antennaria tomentosa* syn. *A. dioica*)

pyramidal bugleweed (*Ajuga pyramidalis*)

Q–R

quack grass (*Agropyron repens*)

Queen-Anne's-lace (*Daucus carota* var. *carota*)

queen-of-the-prairie (*Filipendula rubra*)

ranunculus (*Ranunculus* spp.)

rat tail spruce (*Picea abies* 'Virgata')

red barrenwort (*Epimedium* x *rubrum*)

redbud (*Cercis canadensis*)

red-leaved banana (*Musa zebrina*)

red-twig dogwood (*Cornus alba*)

reed canary grass (*Phalaris arundinacea*)

rhubarb (*Rheum rhabarbarum*)

river birch (*Betula nigra*)

robin-run-away (*Dalibarda repens*)
rock rose (*Cistus* spp.)
rosemary (*Rosmarinus officinalis*)
royal azalea (*Rhododendron schlippenbachii*)
rue (*Ruta graveolens*)
rue anemone (*Anemonella thalictroides*)
rugosa rose (*Rosa rugosa*)
Russian sage (*Perovskia atriplicifolia*)

S

sage (*Salvia officinalis*)
sagittaria (*Sagittaria* spp.)
salvia (*Salvia* spp.)
saucer magnolia (*Magnolia* x *soulangiana*)
scented geraniums (*Pelargonium* spp.)
Scotch pine (*Pinus sylvestris*)
sedum (*Sedum* spp.)
serviceberry (*Amelanchier* spp.)
shadblow (*Amelanchier* spp.)
shasta daisy (*Leucanthemum* x *superbum* syn. *Chrysanthemum* x *superbum* or *C. maximum*)
shooting-star (*Dodecatheon meadia*)
Siberian elm (*Ulmus pumila*)
Siberian iris (*Iris sibirica*)
Siberian swamp iris (*Iris sibirica*)
side-oats grama (*Bouteloua curtipendula*)
silvery glade fern (*Athyrium thelypteroides*)
silver thyme (*Thymus vulgaris* 'Argenteus')
smokebush (*Cotinus coggygria*)
snakeroot (*Cimicifuga racemosa*)
snapdragon (*Antirrhinum majus*)
soapwort (*Saponaria officinalis*, *S. ocymoides*)
Solomon's-plume (*Smilacina* spp.)
Solomon's-seal (*Polygonatum* spp.)
Southern magnolia (*Magnolia grandiflora*)
southernwood (*Artemisia abrotanum*)
spicebush (*Lindera benzoin*)
spider plant (*Chlorophytum comosum*)
spinulose wood fern (*Dryopteris carthusiana*)
spring-beauty (*Claytonia virginica*)
starry false Solomon's seal (*Smilacina stellata*)
stock (*Matthiola incana*)
stokesia (*Stokesia laevis*)
sugar maple (*Acer saccharum*)
sumac (*Rhus* spp.)
summer snowflakes (*Leucojum aestivum*)
summer-sweet (*Clethra alnifolia*)
sunflower (*Helianthus annuus*)
swamp white oak (*Quercus bicolor*)

Swedish ivy (*Plectranthus argentatus*)
sweet alyssum (*Lobularia maritima*)
sweet Annie artemisia (*Artemisia annua*)
sweet basil (*Ocimum basilicum*)
sweet briar or eglantine rose (*Rosa rubiginosa* syn. *R. eglanteria*)
sweet woodruff (*Galium odoratum*)
Swiss stone pine (*Pinus cembra*)
switch grass (*Panicum virgatum*)
sycamore (*Platanus occidentalis*)

T

taro (*Colocasia esculenta* or *Alocasia macrorrhiza*)
Tatarian honeysuckle (*Lonicera tatarica*)
thyme (*Thymus* spp.)
trailing lantana (*Lantana montevidensis*)
trailing nasturtium (*Tropaeolum majus*)
trumpet creeper (*Campsis radicans*)
tulip (*Tulipa* spp.)
tulip tree (*Liriodendron tulipifera*)
turtlehead (*Chelone* spp.)

U–V

umbrella pine (*Sciadopitys verticillata*)
valerian (*Valeriana officinalis*)
variegated Solomon's seal (*Polygonatum odoratum* 'Variegatum')
viburnum (*Viburnum* spp.)
vinca (*Vinca* spp.)
viola (*Viola* spp.)
violet sage (*Salvia nemorosa*)
Virginia bluebells (*Mertensia virginica*)
Virginia creeper (*Parthenocissus quinquefolia*)

W

weeping hemlock (*Tsuga canadensis* 'Pendula')
weeping European beech (*Fagus sylvatica* f. *pendula*)
Welsh onion (*Allium fistulosum*)
white birch (*Betula papyrifera*)
white hellebore (*Veratrum viride*)
white mulberry (*Morus alba*)
white oak (*Quercus alba*)
white pine (*Pinus strobus*)
white poplar (*Populus alba*)
whorled loosestrife (*Lysimachia punctata*)
wild anemone (*Anemone quinquefolia*)
wild bergamot (*Monarda fistulosa*)
wild geranium (*Geranium maculatum*)
wild ginger (*Asarum canadense*)
wild hyacinth (*Camassia scilloides*)

wild lupine (*Lupinus perennis*)
willow bluestar (*Amsonia tabernaemontana*)
willow-leaf sunflower (*Helianthus salicifolius*)
willow-leaved amsonia (*Amsonia hubrectii*)
winterberry holly (*Ilex verticillata*)
winter creeper (*Euonymus fortunei*)
wintergreen (*Gaultheria procumbens*)
winter savory (*Satureja montana*)
wisteria (*Wisteria* spp.)
witch hazel (*Hamamelis* spp.)
wood anemone (*Anemone quinquefolia*)
woodland phlox (*Phlox divaricata*)
wood poppy (*Stylophorum diphyllum*)
woolly veronica (*Veronica incana*)

X–Y–Z

yarrow (*Achillea* spp.)
yellow archangel (*Lamiastrum galeobdolon*)
yellow birch (*Betula lutea*)
yellow mandarin (*Disporum lanuginosum*)
yellow star grass (*Hypoxis hirsuta*)
yellow-twig dogwood (*Cornus stolonifera* 'Flaviramea' and other yellow-stemmed cultivars)
yew (*Taxus* spp.)
zebra grass (*Miscanthus sinensis* 'Zebrinus')
zinnia (*Zinnia elegans, Z. angustifolia*)

INDEX

Bold type signifies photo.

PHOTO CREDITS

Ian Adams: ii, vi, viii, 9, 12, 14, 18, 19, 22, 23, 24, 25, 27, 28, 30, 33, 34, 36, 37, 40, 42, 43, 44, 45, 46, 47, 48, 49, 50, 52, 54, 55 bottom, 56, 57, 58, 59 bottom, 63, 66, 71, 90, 92, 96, 97, 98, 99, 100, 101, 102, 103, 104, 105, 106, 107, 108, 109, 110, 115, 116, 118 top and middle, 119, 121, 124, 125, 129, 131, 138, 139, 140, 141, 144, 146, 148 bottom, 150 bottom, 161, 168, 172, 173, 174, 175, 176, 177, 178, 179, 180, 181, 182, 185, 186 bottom, 188 top, 191 bottom, 195 bottom, 197, 198, 199, 200, 201.

Susan McClure: 2, 3, 4, 6, 7, 8, 10, 11, 13, 16, 17, 20, 21, 26, 29, 32, 38, 39, 55 top, 59 top, 61, 64, 65, 67, 68, 69, 70, 72, 74, 76, 77, 78, 79, 80, 81, 82, 83, 84, 85, 86, 87, 88, 93, 94, 112, 113, 114, 118 bottom, 122, 127, 130, 132, 133, 134, 135, 136, 142, 143, 148 top, 149, 150 top, 151, 152, 153, 154, 155, 156, 157, 158, 159, 162, 163, 164, 165, 166, 171, 184, 186 top, 187, 188 bottom, 189, 190, 191 top, 192, 193, 195 top.